THE DAY I WOKE UP DEAD

CHRIS AND SUSIE MCCOLL

McCollpinkdrink
United States, 2018

Cover Design by Michelle Fairbanks
Edited by Twyla Beth Lambert

Disclaimer: We have tried to recreate events, locales and conversations from our memories of
them. In order to maintain their anonymity in some instances we have changed the names of
individuals and places. We may have changed some identifying characteristics and details such as
physical properties, occupations and places of residence.

ISBN 978-0692176535

We would like to dedicate this book to our kiddos—Tanner, Carson, Maddox & Macy—for putting up with us through all of the good and all of the bad. We love the four of you more than any words could ever express. We pray you would choose to **NOT** follow a path of possible destruction but, instead, be a beacon of light for others.

To all of our family and friends who have supported us through good times and bad, words cannot express how much we love and appreciate you!

And to God—all glory to YOU for anything good in our lives ... and all the bad, we'll blame on Chris.

TABLE OF CONTENTS

Prologue 7

Chapter One: Social Problems 9

Chapter Two: The Most Exciting Rose Ceremony Evaaaaa! ...16

Chapter Three: Beer, Bushes & A Baby 21

Chapter Four: This Calls For Some Self Medicating 28

Chapter Five: Wheel of Fortunes & Failures 36

Chapter Six: Going to Get a Sled 45

Chapter Seven: What About God? 53

Chapter Eight: We Have a Runner! 62

Chapter Nine: Secrets, Secrets, Secrets 73

Chapter Ten: Houston, We Have A "Problem" 84

Chapter Eleven: Lost and Found 92

Chapter Twelve: The Day I Woke Up Dead 102

Chapter Thirteen: Why Me? 111

Chapter Fourteen: How Godronic!! 120

Chapter Fifteen: There's Always Hope 126

About the Authors 136

PROLOGUE

I AWOKE BUT could not seem to get my eyes opened. They felt glued shut.

And my hands, they felt like they weighed 1000 pounds each. I couldn't lift them. Actually, I couldn't even move my body.

And my mouth, my gosh, parched doesn't even begin to tell the story—someone had taken my mouth out, left it in the desert for three weeks and put it back in, dry and cracked.

And why am I sweating like this? Every pore in my body is oozing sweat.

What was happening to me? Did I die?

Was I ... DEAD?

Is this the day I woke up DEAD??

Can you actually wake up dead??

CHAPTER ONE

SOCIAL PROBLEMS

I WAS NERVOUS. It was my first day of class at the University of Oklahoma. I still remember clearly what I was wearing—a long-sleeved chambray shirt tucked into a short, plaid, turquoise skirt with the ever-popular (at the time) brown leather Cole Haan loafers. I had my notebooks neatly titled with my name, and of course, I had the required class books. I was as Type A as they come, and I was ready to get to work.

> I see this girl in front of me and lean over to my buddy and say, "I'm going to marry that girl." Nope, I had never talked to her. Nope, I didn't know a thing about her ... but I knew. I don't know how to explain it but I just KNEW that I was going to marry her.

I vaguely heard a voice behind me say "Susan" as I was watching students file in and find their seats. There it is again, "Susan." I turn to see if maybe someone is talking to me, and sure enough, the guy behind me is staring at me and asks, "Do you have the book for this class?"

I politely tell him, "Yes," and then ask him how he knew my name. He smiled and said, "I read it on your notebook." Oh, duh. I'm sure my face turned beet red and I turned back to the front. He didn't let that stop him though.

"Susan, have you heard this class is really hard? Because that's what I've heard."

Not sure how I responded to his question that day over 26 years ago, but we have laughed many, many times that we met in *that* class. Why? Because it was called, "Social Problems." I just can't even make that up. (For the record, I made a B in that class with the book and studying a LOT. Chris made a C without ever buying the book and with only studying the amount I forced him into.)

> I stalked her after that. I followed her out of the classroom and watched where she went. This was before we had cell phones so I couldn't get her number, and this was well before the world of social media to "follow" her. I just had to try and figure out her schedule and "run into" her as much and as casually as possible.

*   *   *

My freshman year of college was busy. Besides having a full load of classes, I was also working full-time hours at The Gap, plus I had joined a sorority. To say I was busy was putting it mildly. One thing I remember clearly is that I kept running into the guy that sat behind me in Social Problems. It was weird how he was just everywhere I was.

> My fraternity finally had a party that she came to with some of her friends. However, I was a pledge so, if you know anything at all about fraternities, it wasn't like I just got to hang out and enjoy my time. I did, however, get enough time with her to make her laugh a lot.

> She will tell you that it was my ability to make her laugh that made her fall hopelessly in love with

me, but don't let her fool you. It was clearly my dashing good looks.

Now you are probably thinking we started dating after this, right? Nope. In fact, he started dating an older girl on campus. And she was drop-dead gorgeous. I remember feeling insecure when I found out they were dating. It wasn't long before she was calling Chris her "boyfriend" and I figured that I must've been wrong, I guess he didn't actually like me after all. But … turns out he did not feel the same way.

How do I know? Because I vividly recall him TELLING me that right before we shared our FIRST KISS in the parking lot of a party we were at.

After that kiss, we both knew we wanted to be together, but unfortunately, we both already had dates to the same upcoming "date party" (fraternity language)—Chris with the older hot woman and me with a boy that will forever be known as "brown boy" due to some brown pants he wore that Chris made fun of.

Oh yes, "Brown Boy." Stupid brown pants. I still to this day don't know how she could date that loser.

At that party, we finally managed to ditch both of our dates, and we took a cab back to his apartment, laughing all the way. We ended the night in his little twin bed (nothing but kissing happened, mom, dad and kids), giggling about the night and wondering if our dates were going to be mad when, all of a sudden, there was some crazy banging on the window right above our heads.

She was yelling, and at that point, we gave her the nickname of "Psycho Chick."

Somehow, some way, we fell asleep WHILE this was going on. I'm sure the large vats of mystery punch we consumed at the fraternity party had something to do with that.

Imagine my surprise the next day when I went outside my apartment and saw the screen ripped off my window and the metal pieces bent. I'm not gonna lie, I was skeered. I mean, this was rabbit-boiling kind of stuff.

You know, I really think this was the night that started and solidified the "Chris & Susie Against the World" era. He became my person, and I became his from that point on.

We kept doing the college party life thing for a while, but, eventually, just a couple of months after we started dating, we started dreaming of the life beyond all the parties. We had more fun picking up El Chico to go, cuddling on his couch and watching movies than we did going to clubs and doing the party scene. We even started talking about the "M" word (picture me whispering "marriage"). Shoot, Chris had his future kids' names picked out at that point!

Yes, Madison for a girl and Dallas for a boy. Why is it weird that I had kid names picked out while I was in college? Those are cool names.

*   *   *

I think for the sake of understanding the rest of this story, I should touch on the drinking we did while in college. I was a TERRIBLE drinker. Horrible. Got drunk almost every time I drank and ended up crying, yes C-R-Y-I-N-G, on the floor wherever we were. And then I would usually throw up for a while. Good times. Thus, the reason I only drank once or so per week.

Chris, on the other hand, could drink large amounts and just be funnier and happier. He never got sick and he never, hardly ever, passed out. Only when he drank Seagram's 7 & 7, which I quickly outlawed as I didn't like who he became when he drank that.

Unlike me and my once-per-week tragic drinking, Chris drank beer almost every night with whatever fraternity brothers or friends happened to be at his apartment. I was still the super Type A responsible girl who would be up early, have gone to three classes by lunch time, and would be knocking on Chris's apartment door at noon before I had to go work my full-time job at the Gap.

I shared an apartment with my older brother, Tarpley, and we had tinfoil on all our windows to keep that big ball of fire in the sky at bay. Going to class wasn't the most important thing in the world; sleeping in actually kind of was.

Every time I went to his apartment, I would go in and start cleaning up the empty beer cans, pizza boxes and other miscellaneous trash. Cleanliness was not high on their priority list. But, you know, it was college life, and this was just how college boys were. I kind of liked playing the "wife" role and cleaning up things for him.

This is also the first time in my life I learned that you had to actually PAY for water, as there were random cut off notices on their apartment door at any given moment. The one thing they didn't let get cut off was the cable. I mean, they were college boys, and cable went with the pizza and beer.

Back to my pseudo wife role, I also *made* him do his homework and helped him write papers. Oh, gosh, don't even get me started on that.

We had English together second semester. That professor had us write a lot of papers. Instead of me writing my own for this one particular assignment, Susie wrote two. She has always liked to write and just did it. I wasn't going to turn that down!

It was no problem until, one day in class, the professor said, "There is one student that I would like to recognize for an outstanding paper. Chris McColl, please stand up."

And I think the class even applauded me. Except for Susie. She was burning holes into my back with the fire coming from her eyes.

I could not believe it! I wrote two great papers, but he chose to recognize the one I gave Chris!! Ohhhh, I was furious. I cared so much about making good grades, and Chris didn't care at all! This was injustice at its finest. Of course, I probably shouldn't have been doing his work for him, soooo ...

Guess what class I got an "A" in? Yep, English. I honestly hardly ever even went to that class.

*   *   *

So we ended our first year of college together. Marriage became a bigger and bigger topic. We spent ALL of our spare time together. He was my yin and I was his yang. The term "soulmates" started to make sense.

I was still working at The Gap, and one of my coworkers started talking about how her neighbors were abusing a dog and how she was going to rescue (aka: steal) it. Naturally I told Chris about it.

I told Susie to tell her coworker we wanted it! A dog! Exactly what we needed.

Operation "Save the Dog" went into effect and my coworker ended up bringing me the dog. I immediately took her to Chris's apartment.

As I walked past his window, he happened to look out and yelled, "I said a dog, not a horse." Apparently, Paisley was bigger than he expected.

It became apparent pretty quickly that his apartment was not the perfect home for sweet Paisley, nor were busy, irresponsible college students the perfect parents. Luckily, we took her to visit his family, and they quickly fell in love with her. They loved on her for many years from that point on, and Paisley went from the abused life to a life of love and pampering.

Having Paisley, although for a short-lived time, was a turning point in our relationship. We realized that we wanted our own dog, but with that dog we would need a house and a yard. With that house we would need to be married. So first, we went ring shopping, and then the house hunting began.

CHAPTER TWO

THE MOST EXCITING ROSE CEREMONY EVAAAAA!

I TOLD CHRIS that I thought it would be cool if he proposed to me on the top of the Ferris wheel at the State Fair of Oklahoma. For some reason, this seemed romantic to me at the time, I guess. Although, have you ever been to a state fair??? "Romantic" is not a term I would choose to describe it now.

> I had the ring but I certainly couldn't propose the way Susie wanted me to. Where would the WOW factor be in that? I had to come up with a way that she wouldn't suspect ...

One day, I showed up at his apartment, as we had made plans of some sort. When I walked in the door, I immediately saw rose petals scattered on the floor in a trail toward his bedroom. I followed the trail, which led to his room. There were more rose petals leading to his bathroom. I got mad!!! Why were there rose petals?? Had a girl been in his room??

> I laughed at her. "You think I had a girl over and she was spinning around throwing rose petals???"

He flung open the bathroom door, and on the shower door he had written in shaving cream, "Will You Marry Me?" I started laughing, and we hugged, kissed and I said, "YES!" He presented me with my ring, and I couldn't believe it when I put it on. It was just perfect.

I told you I'd marry this girl.

Now came the hard part. We had to tell my parents. His parents were easy—they loved me. We spent a lot of time with them, and I think they knew this was coming. Mine were a different story. My parents were actually going through a divorce at the time, so it wasn't the happiest of times. Leading up to this, my mom had accepted Chris, but my dad wouldn't really even hardly speak to him. I think it's hard for any dad to think of his little girl with a man.

I wouldn't say her dad was "cold" to me. I'd say he was more "freezing" or "subzero."

So, we told them. And they did try to give us a word of warning that getting married as young as we were wouldn't be easy. We were 19 and 21 at the time of our engagement. Honestly, there was nothing anyone could have said to us to talk us out of getting married. Our young minds were made up.

As far as planning the wedding, well, we aren't the best of planners. I mentioned flying to Vegas and getting married there, but Chris's momma put an end to that real fast. We got engaged in September, found a house we could afford on a VA loan (so we didn't have to have a big down payment) in the next couple of months, and pulled the trigger on the wedding. I still remember planning the wedding day like it was yesterday.

My mom pretty much took over. We told her we were closing on the house on January 6th, so we wanted to get married before then. She freaked out, as that only gave a couple of weeks' notice.

She was on the phone with the church, asking us details we didn't know. How many people are coming? No idea. What day do you want it? Don't care. Who will be in your wedding party? Do we have to have one?

You get the picture.

Luckily, Chris's mom got the wedding plans in motion as I didn't have a clue as to how to do that. My mom helped me shop for a dress and, true to my "always loves a deal" self, I found a dress on sale for $100!!

She was telling people how much things cost even back then!

It wasn't fancy, which also fit my practical, non-fancy self. We got the flowers and cake from Homeland, a local grocery store that I called the "One Stop Wedding Shop."

I laugh looking back at this time and the wedding arrangements because it is still so who I am. I don't ever understand making a big deal out of things. I like practical. I like simple. I don't need a lot of pomp and ceremony. Truthfully, if we were to renew our vows and have another "wedding," I'd choose to be outside either on a beach overlooking the ocean or in a pretty field surrounded by trees and God's beauty.

The night before the wedding, the last night in my childhood home, my mom pulled me aside and said, "You can tell me if you're pregnant—is that why you are getting married so quickly?"

I just laughed at her and said, "No mom! I'm not pregnant! We are just ready to start our life together. Not to mention, we bought a house!"

We got married on January 7th, 1993, at 4:00 in the afternoon. It was a Thursday. Apparently, that was the first time the church had an opening in their parlor. We had about 30 of our closest family and friends there. It was a nice ceremony and accomplished what we needed. And like I said before, I KNEW I was going to marry this chick.

We left right after our wedding ceremony for our honeymoon trip.

We planned the honeymoon just about as well as we planned our wedding ... not much planning at all. No hotel reservations, no plans at all really. We just knew we wanted to go to Eureka Springs, Arkansas, a quaint little town that would be perfect for a few nights' get away.

We took off in my 1990 burgundy Honda Accord onto which someone, I think Chris's sisters, had shaving creamed "Just Married" and tied some cans to the back of it.

About an hour out of town, we saw flashing lights behind us, and Chris pulled the car over. The officer was nice and let us go with a warning to slow down.

About another hour later, we heard sirens and saw flashing lights again, and Chris pulled over yet again. This time, Chris got out of the car.

I told that officer, "Sir, I'm sorry if I was speeding—we just got married!"

He responded with this: "Son, I can't do anything worse to you than you've already done to yourself. Slow it down and good luck."

When Chris got back in the car, I said, "Well, did you get a ticket?" He grinned and handed me a piece of paper, "Put that in my warning pile."

Next, we stopped at an El Chico Mexican restaurant to have our "fancy" honeymoon dinner. (We were super loyal to our favorite restaurants even back then!) When the waitress found out we had just gotten married a few hours earlier, they comped our meal! At 19 and 21 years old, we felt like we had won the lottery!! We drove on to Eureka Springs, only to show up and find a town ... basically deserted.

Swell.

Turns out Eureka Springs, a hot Christmas vacation spot, pretty much shuts completely down in January. Who knew?

Luckily, I found my beautiful new bride a really awesome cabin complete with a HOT TUB in the middle of it—INSIDE the cabin. I scored some major bonus points for that one! The manager even served us hot, fresh chocolate chip cookies since we were newlyweds. What more do you need to make a honeymoon awesome?

Over the next couple of days, we rode horses through a beautiful wooded forest, we shopped in cute antique stores, and we pretty much just basked in the fact that we were FINALLY married. We had finally made official what we had felt since first meeting.

We were finally Mr. & Mrs. McColl.

Only ... don't call us that because that sounds OLLLLD. Just call us Chris & Suz.

CHAPTER THREE

BEER, BUSHES & A BABY

HONESTLY, WE COULDN'T wait to get home from our honeymoon and start our life together in our brand-new house! Well, brand new to us, anyways. This house was red brick, white paint, corner lot. It had red carpet, pink countertops and apple wallpaper in the kitchen. We thought it was PERFECT. No kids at that point yet, so of course the house seemed HUGE to us. We didn't think we'd ever be able to fill it!

> Not too long after we moved into our new house, my brother Tarpley came over and we might have downed quite a few beers. Later that night, it seemed like a good idea to tie sheets around our shoulders as capes and go rollerblading through the neighborhood. This incident might be part of the reason that all of our neighbors thought we were the kids of the people who bought our house.

Man, did we have great times in that house! Of course, we quickly got a black Labrador Retriever we named Rocky. He was technically our first baby. Not too long after we got him, we decided he was probably lonely and got another lab we named Buddy. He was a yellow lab and the sweetest dog to ever live. Rocky and Buddy were our *life*. Our house was next

to a big field full of cows, so we got to let the dogs run out
there almost every day.

Eventually, Chris made friends with our neighbor, Greg,
who taught him how to hunt. It was cool because they could
go right out our front door to the field and hunt for geese!

And quail.

*   *   *

Chris started working full-time, selling door chimes. He
made a very good living for us, especially at our age,
although it was door-to-door sales and definitely not the
most stable income. If you know anything at all about door-
to-door sales, it speaks volumes about Chris that he was so
good at it at such a young age.

I wasn't always good at it. As a matter of fact, I
got FORCED into it by my father, Bruce McColl,
who was a selling machine. I was super excited
around high school graduation time because all
of my friends were receiving amazing gifts from
their parents—cars, trips ... you get the picture. I
couldn't possibly imagine how extravagant MY
gift was going to be—I mean, come on, I did have
a C- average after all.

Shortly before the big day, my dad calls me into
his office. "Son, I'm super proud of you and so
excited about the next chapter in your life. The gift
I'm giving you will help shape, mold and prepare
you for future success in life."

I can see out of the corner of my eye a stack of
cardboard boxes about waist high. I was so
curious! WHAT has he gotten me? What's in these

mysterious boxes? Is it GOLD? PILES OF CASH? My mind was racing—the possibilities were endless!

So, my dad grabs one of the cardboard boxes, sets it on his desk, and opens it up. He pulls out a small, brown, plastic rectangular box that fit in his hand. "Son, this is a door chime. I'm going to teach you how to sell this to small businesses. The market potential is endless."

Doorbells??? Selling? Work?? My dad is giving me WORK for my graduation gift?? My friends are getting elaborate gifts and I get ... WORK???

Of course, as an 18-year-old, I couldn't see the value in this gift then, but looking back, it was the best gift I ever could've received. It truly did shape and mold me into the person I am today. You know, like TEACHING a person to fish is better than just giving them the fish.

I had started working full-time for my grandpa's roofing company and was continuing going to school. In the evenings, I would work on homework and Chris would go play golf, fish, hunt or whatever activity the season called for.

(Let me interject a bit of marital advice here: Do NOT change the "rules" for your spouse when you get married. If they spent a lot of time golfing or fishing or whatever hobby they did while you were dating, do NOT expect them to stop when you get married!! I know so many couples that do this! And it leads to a big ol' fat cup of bitterness and unhappiness. You should ENCOURAGE one another to do the things you LOVE to do. Trust me when I say this will lead to happiness and fulfillment!)

When together at home, we would eat frozen pizzas, take-out Chinese, or Chris would cook something on the grill. Chris drank Keystone Light, and that was my era of box wine, every single night. We watched every new movie that came out, both in the theatre and on video. VCRs were a pretty big deal back then! I hate to think of how lazy we would've been if Netflix Unlimited streaming would have been an option!

> Because we were the only ones married amongst our friends, our house quickly became the "hangout" spot. We would grill, play games, sit out on the back porch, and talk about life.
>
> And drink.
>
> A lot.
>
> Susie wasn't a big drinker, so she'd always eventually go to bed ... but me and my friends? Well, we could stay up the whole night. One night, we all decided to shave our heads. Let's just say, if you and your college-age buddies decide to drink a lot, hide the hair clippers!

I couldn't believe my eyes when I woke up. There was Chris next to me ... bald as a baby's bottom. You know how some guys look really great with the shaved look? Ummm, not Chris. I was really not a happy wife. Not only that, but the house was a disaster. There were beer cans and piles of hair everywhere.

> My friends and I convinced ourselves that night that if we shaved our heads, everyone would think we looked like PILOTS. And anyone and everyone knows that pilots are cool—ummm, hello, *Top Gun*.
>
> Turns out ... we looked like idiots, and I like having hair.

*   *   *

To explain to you just how young we were when we got married, one Saturday morning, I was lying on the couch, horribly hungover from whatever escapade we had participated in the night before, eating Chips Ahoy cookies and watching *Saved by The Bell*. If you do not know what this show is, the fact that it was on the same time as Saturday morning cartoons is sufficient information to let you know that I was still basically a child.

Anywhoooooo ... after I was finished with my gluten-, sugar- and fat-filled GMO, non-organic breakfast of chocolate chip cookies dipped in milk, I sat the package (because I didn't see a need for portion control at age 19, I guess) on the floor next to the couch and took a nice mid-morning nap. When I woke up, I picked up the package of cookies and my now empty cup of milk and proceeded to walk to the window and look out lovingly at our brand new backyard with pride.

As I was looking out the window, I felt something creepy crawly on my arms and looked down to find .... A MILLION ANTS CRAWLING ALL OVER ME, the cookie package, and the cup.

I screamed, threw down the package and cup, and ran to the ... shower. It was the only reasonable place in my mind to escape the vicious attack ants that had invaded our home.

Susie called me up, screaming in hysteria. I was on the golf course with my brother Tarpley, and we both thought she had been attacked. Turns out she had been ... by ANTS.

She wanted to move.

I'm not even joking.

Seriously, I was ready to pack my bags. I was sad that we'd have to leave our new house, but clearly, I could not live on top of what must've been the biggest ant farm in Oklahoma history.

We fought those ants for years. And the ants pretty much won.

*   *   *

Our very first New Year's Eve as a married couple rolled around. One of our other friend couples had gotten married by this point, and they invited us to their house for the night's festivities. After a long night of playing games and drinking, we got back to our own home around 2 a.m.

I recall quite vividly that as we opened the back door, we were instantly met by our house alarm blaring loudly and our two labs running around the house in a tizzy.

Upon further inspection, it seemed the house alarms had been going off since we left and the noise upset the dogs so much that they had diarrhea all over the inside of the house. Like, I'm talking running around THE ENTIRE HOUSE having massive diarrhea. I've never seen a mess like it. Luckily, we had that *dark red* carpet.

We spent our first hours of 1994 on our hands and knees with buckets of soapy water cleaning up pile upon pile of dog poo.

I'm pretty sure Susie blamed that whole mess on me for setting the alarm on "away" mode instead of "home mode." I will say, I never made that mistake again.

*   *   *

We had so much fun "playing house" those first couple of years of marriage. We planted flowers, trees, learned how to take care of our yard properly. Our across-the-street neighbor, Bill, became pretty much like a father figure to us. He taught us all sorts of things and loaned us all sorts of tools and gadgets that we didn't even know existed.

* * *

I really wanted to have kids, but Susie kept saying no. She had to "finish school first." One day, we were at Walmart and she needed to buy her birth control pills. I knew she really wanted certain bushes for the front yard, so I told her, "If you don't buy the birth control pills, we can buy the bushes instead." We were on a pretty tight budget.

At first, she didn't go for it, but after I convinced her that it would probably take at least a year or so to get pregnant, she conceded.

I was pregnant the very next month. I would've been mad at Chris, but I was too ecstatic about the thought of having OUR BABY that I only cried tears of joy and immediately began planning our soon-to-be baby's room! A deep love that I didn't even know could exist began the moment I knew a little human was growing inside of me!!

I had no idea how much buying bushes could change our lives!

CHAPTER FOUR

THIS CALLS FOR SOME SELF MEDICATING

OTHER THAN ENDURING awful "morning" sickness for approximately three months, I loved being pregnant. I would like to take a moment and express my annoyance at whomever named it "morning" sickness. I'm sure it was a man, as that is just an outright lie —I was sick ALLLLLLLL day long. I was still going to school and working full-time at my grandpa's roofing company.

My super healthy daily lunch was SweeTARTS and Cheetos from the vending machine at work. (That baby is now a strapping 6'4" muscular man, so I guess it worked out okay.)

I can remember being so tired I would literally fall asleep at my desk. Luckily, my Pop didn't fire me!

I can also remember during this time that my "morning" sickness was so bad I actually threw up into my hands walking out of a class at the University of Central Oklahoma. Every college student's dream, I'm sure.

Once I made it through the early stages of sickness, my appetite kicked in like never before. I could down an entire footlong Philly cheese steak sandwich, chips and cookie like no one's business. Eating a whole pizza by myself became a given. Somehow, I only gained 29 pounds during my pregnancy, but guess who gained even more?

At one point of this weight gain, I was convinced I must be pregnant too.

*   *   *

This is probably a great time to bring up our less than wise financial decisions. There was no Dave Ramsey back then, I'm just sayin'. When we got married, we both had paid-for cars. I had a burgundy Honda Accord EX that my parents graciously gave me, and Chris had a blue Datsun 280ZX with blinds on the back window.

Those weren't BLINDS. They were louvers. That car was awesome.

Rather than be content with our debt-free car status, we decided to buy not one, but *two* new cars and take out nice, hefty loans on top of the home mortgage we had just recently taken on, as well. We could rationalize debt like no one's business.

The first car we bought on our own, the deal was so bad that the finance manager "threw in" the warranty. The finance manager had to call us back into the office three times to lower the interest rate because it was illegal to charge as much as they were charging us.

At this point, car buying became something of a "hobby" for us. If a tag was expiring or the vehicle needed tires, I would just go purchase a new vehicle. I mean, it had new tires anyways.

You don't realize until you trade vehicles several times how much negative equity one can actually build up. I'm pretty sure we set some kind of record. I was definitely no financial guru and was, unfortunately, learning through my own poor decisions.

We also bought a speedboat just a couple of months prior to my due date. For some reason, I went along with this but didn't think it was a great idea being that (a) I was hugely pregnant; and (b) it was definitely not a kid-friendly boat. I remember saying that I didn't know how much we would actually get to use it.

> There was no "we," but there was a whole lot of ME. This was actually my plan. A hidey-hole. I now had a place to get away quickly from my crazy-hormone-infested young wife.

*   *   *

So back to the baby ... every minute of every day was spent in preparation for this new little life!! The first grand baby for both sets of grandparents, the first nephew for all of our siblings ... we all couldn't wait for his arrival!

*   *   *

One night, we were sound asleep and I woke up to a really wet bed. I was lying there wondering if I had wet the bed, the dog had wet the bed, or if my water had broken. I woke Chris up and said, "The sheets are all wet—do you think my water broke?"

The problem with this scenario was that I didn't FEEL anything gushing from me like I thought I would, but ... just to be safe, we went to the hospital.

> Apparently, the dog or I peed the bed. And I'm going with the dog. Her water was still intact.

A week or so later, the day finally arrived. I was strangely restless all day long and, for some crazy reason, I was suddenly craving PEA SALAD and insisted Chris make it for my dinner. He is the cook in the relationship.

Pea Salad? Pea Salad? Pea Freaking Salad.

"You want me to make pea salad? Like with mayonnaise and stuff?" I asked.

For the record, mayonnaise is clearly from the devil. But, of course, I whipped up the greatest pea salad west of the Mississippi.

A bit later, before I could even eat said salad, I was watching my then-fave TV show, *Beverly Hills 90210*, when I started feeling major contractions. We timed them and eventually decided it really was time to go the hospital.

My labor was long and, unfortunately, I started throwing up in the hospital. Every time I would throw up, I would also then wet the entire bed. I was so embarrassed by this betrayal of my body that, rather than bother the TRAINED NURSE to help me, I made Chris do it. Of course, I had an epidural (I made sure to PLAN that!!), so I couldn't actually feel my lower body and poor Chris had to hoist me over, remove the huge wet pad and then shove the new dry pad underneath me.

Of course, I was young and still wasn't sure what I was going to do with my life career-wise, so male nurse became a short, brief consideration.

It has always, always been Chris & Me Against the World. He has always had my back and he is my ride or die.

My firstborn son, Tanner Allan McColl, was born on May 18, 1995. The game had changed. The responsibilities levels were raised. The fear of the unknown and the idea that I had absolutely no idea what I was doing became a reality. Our lives

became ALL ABOUT THE BABY, and guess what?
The dogs no longer slept with us.

Having a baby was a little harder than we expected.
Nobody warned me that it might hurt to go to the bathroom
after having a baby, and certainly nobody warned me that you
should probably take a stool softener. This is my PSA to all
women who have not had a baby yet but might possibly in the
future—you NEED a stool softener. Trust me, as I spent hours
in the bathroom crying while there was family over to see the
new baby. There I was, stuck on the commode in complete
misery while everyone else was ooohing and awwwing in the
other room over the little life that I had JUST GIVEN BIRTH
TO! This was probably one of the first moments in motherhood
that I realized life was no longer about me.

I also didn't know that my boobs would HURT when my
milk came in! No one told me that! I can remember looking
over at Chris soundly sleeping while I was sitting up in bed
with these strangely painful, HARD boobs, just crying my
eyes out. And he didn't even wake up!!

I can remember wanting to throw something at his head.

If she had just woke me up, not only would I have
been more than willing to help, I would have
gladly assisted with new hard-boob relief. I was
practically a male nurse after all.

We made it through those initial few hard weeks with a
newborn and settled into a pretty easy routine. I had quit my
job and was a new stay-at-home mom. Chris had started a job
at a car dealership and, although he worked a lot of hours, he
made a considerable amount of money, so things were pretty
smooth. Tanner was a really, really easy baby, taking at least a
3-hour nap during the day and sleeping through the night
before he was even six weeks old.

I remember telling Susie, "Having a baby is so easy. We could raise our own village." These words became a running joke between us because just 21 months later, we had our second son, Carson Andrew McColl, and he was anything but easy.

Colic, acid reflux, projectile spit-up, and he didn't sleep through the night until he was about 18 months old. I spent a lot of time bouncing him around the house or sitting him in his car seat on the running dryer next to the also also-running vacuum. Other than driving him around in the car, which we did a LOT, these were the only things that soothed him.

Did you know you could actually SLEEP on a speedboat?

*   *   *

Chris was working a LOT of hours during this time, and I remember being completely overwhelmed and feeling like a failure as a mother. At the time, we went to a family practitioner, and rather than putting our son on medication for acid reflux, she put ME on Prozac. She told me, "Susie, it's normal for babies to cry and spit up."

So Susie got the Prozac and I started "self-medicating" by upping my adult beverage consumption.

Being that I was only 23 at the time and NOT A DOCTOR, I believed her and went along with it for a while. I'm not sure if the Prozac helped or not, but soon after, I changed to a pediatrician who finally addressed Carson's health problems. I took myself off of the Prozac.

I learned a valuable lesson that, just because a doctor says something, doesn't mean it's automatically the truth. You have to be your own, and your children's own, health advocate.

*   *   *

It was during this really tough time as new, overwhelmed parents that we decided to up and move to Alabama to live closer to Chris's parents.

Honestly, this time is kind of a blur in my head. Chris quit his job at the car dealership and went back to selling door chimes door-to-door, and that required him to travel out of town. And that meant I was home alone in a new state with two little ones. Not ideal. We had rented this little old house that we quickly learned was full of what we came to not so lovingly call "Big Bugs."

> One morning, I woke up and felt a tickle sensation in my hair. As I started to gain consciousness from a Long Island Iced tea-induced coma, I realized that this tickling was, in fact, one of these enormous BLACK BUGS. IN. MY. HAIR.
>
> My man instincts kicked in and in a quick, single motion, I swept the giant dinosaur-bug off my head into my hand and did what any normal loving husband would do … I proceeded to SPIKE the Big Bug against Susie's sleeping back as I screamed, "Die, you giant beast, DIE!!!"
>
> Needless to say, that was the end of ME ever sleeping in THAT bed again.

*   *   *

Speaking of Long Island Iced Tea comas, it was during this time in Alabama that we started the "Happy Hour" trend. Every evening we'd go to Chris's parents' house and have either margaritas or Long Island Ice Teas. This would usually result in me basically passing out by 7 p.m. and both of us gaining about 20 pounds over a couple month period.

We had rented our house from an older gentleman who seemed like a nice enough fellow ... until one day, he came into the house unannounced and caught me in my bra and panties. I guess he saw Chris's car leave and thought I had left with him and no one would be inside the home. To this day we wonder if there's any secretly recorded videos by our landlord floating around the internet.

This new revelation that our landlord knew no boundaries plus the big black bugs did it. I called my brother and said, "Tarpley, good news, we are coming home. Bad news, you have to move out of our house." Tarpley had rented our home from us while we were in Alabama. He has always had my back and was glad I was coming back to be close to him.

We were really, really happy to be back in Oklahoma. Moving hadn't solved any of our problems or reduced any of our stress, but it did help us realize that Oklahoma would always be our HOME.

CHAPTER FIVE

WHEEL OF FORTUNES & FAILURES

WE WERE SO happy to be back in Oklahoma. It will always be HOME to us. There might not be that many exciting things "to do" in Oklahoma, but man, the people are pretty awesome and it's a good place to raise a family.

Chris went back to the car dealership and, although he was a great salesman, he really hated the hours. Many days he wouldn't get home until after the kids were already in bed and I was ready to go to bed. He never got a whole weekend off, only a Sunday. It was really hard on our family life.

I got a little part time job teaching Mother's Day Out that gave us a much-needed discount for our two growing boys to be in preschool. I loved being at the school and teaching the young kids, and it at least got me out of the house and around other adults two days per week, which I really needed.

We also decided during this time that we would go ahead and have one more baby. It didn't take us long before we were pregnant with our third.

The only problem with being back in Oklahoma was that the problems that we had before we moved were still there, waiting for us upon our return. We were still in debt, living check to check, and this basically just became our way of life.

So, of course, like most logical, thinking adults, we decided to go ahead and have another kid and buy a bigger, more expensive house.

That should definitely help alleviate some of our stress.

*   *   *

One day, I left my job at the preschool to run home and check the mailbox at lunchtime. I had recently tried out for *The Wheel of Fortune* at our local mall and was waiting anxiously every day for a letter telling me if I made it onto the show or not. Chris and I played the game every night, and being that we are SLIGHTLY competitive, it became a huge part of our lives. It was truly my DREAM to be on the *Wheel of Fortune*.

As luck would have it, that particular day, there WAS a letter from *Wheel of Fortune*!! I was so excited and a bit confused because, instead of being addressed to ME, it was addressed to Chris. Nevertheless, I ripped it open and began excitedly reading ... only to figure out that I had NOT made it on the show. CHRIS had.

Now, I would love to say that I was happy for him, but I truly wasn't. I was actually mad and even cried myself to sleep over it that night. Poor guy, he was excited but couldn't even enjoy it as he knew that I was incredibly disappointed. I acted terribly, and imagine how DUMB I felt the next day when ANOTHER letter from *Wheel of Fortune* came, this time addressed to ME.

Yep, I had made it on as well.

Holy Moly, I would've been screwed if she didn't make it on too!

Chris got to go on the show first, and he won $2,600. Not exactly the windfall we had hoped for, especially because we had just bought a new, bigger house and needed quite a bit of furniture to fill it.

Susie cried in our hotel room after I only won $2,600. She said it wasn't over the money, that she was missing the kids, but I'm pretty certain if I had won $50,000, she wouldn't have been crying.

Right after we got home from taping the show, we excitedly moved into our new home, and I think she reminded me DAILY that if I had just known Billy Bob Thornton and Angelina Jolie were dating, we could've furnished the entire house.

And then it was my turn. I won $11,200, which was enough to get me to the bonus round. In the bonus round, I was given two words and the category was a "thing." If you are familiar with the show at all, you know they give you R, S, L, N, T and E. So, my puzzle looked like this:

"_ _ N_ _ _ _ _"

In addition, I guessed a "K," so when the buzzer started the count down for me to solve it, the puzzle looked like this:

"_ _ N K _ _ _ _"

Yep, only 2 letters.

Literally, the first thing out of my mouth (and I have video to prove it) was "JUNK FOOD??"

That was right, and the next thing you know, you see me jumping up and down enthusiastically, bear-hugging Pat Sajak. It is really hysterical, if you watch it, because he puts his hands on my shoulders to try to stop me from jumping as I was actually 7-1/2 months pregnant at the time.

Oh, and if you are wondering what I won, it was CASH in the amount of twenty-five thouuuuuuusand dolllllllllllars!!

And, NO, it was not staged. I really am just that great of a *Wheel of Fortune* contestant!!!

> I was happy she won, but I knew I was never going to live that down.

*   *   *

Our new house was awesome. And we were able to furnish it and landscape it with MY winnings! It was the smallest house in the neighborhood, but we were just so ecstatic to be there because we had driven through that neighborhood so many times over the years, dreaming of living there.

The area had an awesome pond where Chris taught the boys how to fish and there was a neighborhood pool for me to spend the summer days with them at. I cannot even tell you how many cumulative hours were spent at that pond and that pool.

Just a couple of months after moving in, the Lord blessed us with our third son, Maddox Christopher McColl.

> Angelina Jolie actually STOLE the name Maddox from us. I'm not even kidding. When my Wheel episode taped, I told the audience that we were having our third son and naming him "Maddox." Angelina adopted a son soon after that and named him Maddox.

> Remember, the puzzle I lost on was "Angelina Jolie and Billy Bob Thornton." We are pretty certain her publicist sent her the video tape of the show and she thought, "Look at this incredibly HANDSOME guy and what a cool name he's naming his baby—Maddox."

> So, there you have it, I pretty much gave Angelina her baby's name. You're welcome, Angelina.

*   *   *

For the next 12 years, we had the picture-perfect family lifestyle, living in our new neighborhood. We made great friends with neighbors, and the kids had plenty of friends to spend late summer nights outside with, catching frogs and riding scooters and bikes. We had an annual neighborhood 4th of July parade, pool party and cookout. There was tons of fishing, swimming and fun.

Life was good.

Except ... I started noticing that Chris was drinking more and more.

As I mentioned before, drinking had always been a normal part of our lives. But it seemed like he was drinking earlier in the evenings and drinking larger amounts. I mentioned to him that I thought he needed to cut back, and he got pretty defensive and told me that "everyone" drinks beer to unwind and relax. Which, honestly, they did.

> Susie started bugging me about my drinking and I would tell her to "chill out." I mean, my gosh, I'd been busting my butt all day at work and I deserved to come home and unwind with a couple of beers. Or maybe a 12-pack.

> It's not like she didn't know I drank a lot of beer when she married me! I wasn't suddenly going to change now!

*   *   *

Throughout these years, our boys were all on competitive baseball teams. Now, if you don't know what that means, you haven't had a kid in competitive sports lately. When I was growing up, you might "play soccer" or you might "do gymnastics." But, now? For TODAY'S kids? Well, if you aren't on a competitive team by the time you are 5 years old, your career as a professional athlete is pretty well doomed. Okay, I exaggerate a little, but not much.

Our boys were all very athletic so we literally spent every single night and weekend at the ballpark playing baseball games and tournaments. Oh, they also played soccer, basketball and football, but the majority of the time was spent playing baseball. By the time our fourth baby and only girl, Macy Elizabeth McColl, was 6 weeks old, she had literally been to 36 baseball games. Thus is the life of a fourth child born in late May to a baseball-crazed family.

> I was such a fanatic about my boys and baseball that if there was a tournament on a given weekend that got rained out, I would literally sit and pout like a two-year-old because "we" couldn't play that weekend!

*   *   *

Our family's love of sports also began to make it abundantly clear that the car dealership life was just not going to work. I can remember Chris running up to the fields in his "work pants," trying to catch the games, and I just hated it because he loved being there so much.

He began looking for work elsewhere and eventually ended up selling mortgages for a mortgage company. Mortgage life was awesome compared to car sales life because he had normal 8-to-5 hours and Chris was actually able to start not only ATTENDING all of the kids' games, but also COACHING them. I so loved that he wanted to coach them! He was, and IS to this day, such a great dad.

Actually, mortgages didn't interest me at all. I was interested in the INCOME I could earn by selling mortgages, but the idea of sitting behind a desk with a tie on, dealing with paperwork and numbers was truthfully my worst nightmare. However, this gig also got me the title of "Coach," which I truly loved!

*   *   *

We became really good friends with all of the other baseball parents, and we spent a lot of time hanging out with them, both at the ballpark and at each other's houses in between games. Our core group all loved to drink, play poker, and basically have a good time. We'd go out of town for tournaments, and the dads would stay up all hours of the night having a good ol' drunken time.

I, being the responsible parent, would get the kids into bed and ready for the games the next day.

Sometimes the baseball games actually got in the way of our fun! Man, those were some awesome times with great friends! We truly had a blast together. And truthfully, some of those late-night poker games funded the McColl family baseball traveling expense account!

*   *   *

Now, it was also during this time that I got rather sick and stayed sickly for several years. I had chronic strep throat and needed my tonsils out, but because I was busy being pregnant and nursing my 3rd and 4th babies (born 19 months apart), I could never make time for the surgery. I was so sick that I'm really not sure how Baby #4 ever got made, but I guess I had one good day!!

It was absolutely awful being chronically sick. I felt rundown, tired, no energy and just "blah" all the time. Not only did I have chronic strep throat, but I also started having chronic sinus infections and chronic "bladder" infections. I am putting "bladder" in quotes because that's what *I* called them, but the doctors didn't really know WHAT to call them. The doctors were pretty puzzled by all of my issues and just kept putting me on antibiotics. I know, at one point, I even took one antibiotic for six months straight.

I tell you all of this to tell you that I did not really have enough energy to pay attention to Chris's growing drinking problem. I just didn't. I had four little kids, aged 8 down to newborn, that literally needed me from sunup to sundown. When Chris would assure me that "everyone" drank that much, it was simply much easier to just agree with him then to try and battle him.

Over the next few years we would have MANY, MANY discussions (read, "fights") about his drinking. Sometimes they would be met with defensiveness, and sometimes he would agree he needed to cut back ... and he would. For a while, anyways.

This drinking conversation was getting old.

It's weird because, initially, when Susie started mentioning that I was drinking too much, I meant it when I told her that I didn't have a problem. I was simply doing what I had always done.

Even growing up, my family drank at every opportunity. At every get-together or family event, drinking would happen to some level. So, of course, me drinking was NORMAL. Me not drinking would never be normal.

But, secretly, I had started to notice a constant increase in the amounts that I was drinking, and this was something that did, in fact, concern me.

But I certainly wasn't going to tell her that!

CHAPTER SIX

GOING TO GET A SLED

ONE MORNING, I was driving my oldest son, Tanner, to school. He was 12 at the time and in middle school. It was only about a 5-minute drive, but, boy, EVERYTHING changed in that short five minutes.

Tanner: "Mom, it's Dare Week at school. It's all about drugs."

Me: "Oh, really? I bet that is interesting."

Tanner: "It is. Did you know that they say alcohol is a drug?" (in kind of an accusing tone, if I remember correctly).

Me: "Well, yes, technically it is because you can actually become addicted to it. But, it's weird because it's LEGAL to drink alcohol once you turn 21 and are an adult. You just don't want to drink too much. Like me, I can drink a glass of wine and, obviously, that is fine."

Tanner: "Well, Dad drinks A LOT of beer. A LOT."

At this point I kind of remember panicking in my head about what to say, and I think I finally just agreed and said, "Yes, he does."

Tanner: "I mean, he drinks when we go fishing, when we play golf, when we go hunting ... He drinks every night. That's a lot."

Me: "You are right, Tanner. He does drink a lot and I think he definitely needs to cut way back."

It's interesting, Tanner is now 23 and he doesn't even remember that conversation. But for me? That conversation is BURNED into my memory because it was a major turning point for me. I knew right then and there that I was going to have to take a stand and INSIST Chris do something about his drinking. We had done the "You are drinking too much" thing and him placating me with, "I'll cut back," for years, and that obviously was not working.

And now the kids were being affected—they were definitely taking NOTICE of Chris's alcohol habits. And my goodness, even more worrisome, the kids were LEARNING from him. Everyone knows that boys learn from their dads and want to emulate them. I certainly didn't want my then soon-to-be-teenagers (ages 12 and 10 at the time) picking up bad drinking habits at an early age.

All day long, I worried about what I would say to Chris when he got home. I dreaded this conversation. DREADED it. If you know me at all, you know I'm pretty much a professional "conflict avoider." I like HAPPY. I like everyone getting along. I do not like fights, disagreements or any kind of disharmony, especially in my own family. Can't everyone just get along???

But, I knew it had to be done.

I waited until I got the kids all in bed, and then I approached him as he laid back in his brown leather recliner, watching television and drinking a beer.

I honestly cannot remember the exact words I said, but I do know that I told him about Dare Week at school and the conversation that Tanner had started with me about his drinking. I also know that I was crying.

I feel like this is a good time to remind you all of Chris's and my relationship up to that point in our lives: It was always Chris & Susie Against the World, and suddenly I felt like I was betraying that sacred trust. Like I was suddenly against him.

I know that might sound strange, but that is how I felt. We were ALWAYS on each other's side.

Did I tell you that Chris basically saved my life? He did. This was before we got married, while we were still dating. We went on a spring break "skiing" trip with some of our friends. I use the term "skiing" loosely, though, because, honestly, not a lot of skiing actually happened.

When I booked that condo, the travel agent failed to tell me one key ingredient—the ski resort was CLOSED. It had gone bankrupt and was no longer in operation. No wonder I got such a great deal on that condo!

The first night we were there, everyone drank quite a bit and got pretty rowdy. I remember feeling annoyed at their state of mind and decided at that point to go to bed.

We decided to fire up the grill to cook some chicken but, dang, it was really cold outside and really windy, so we decided to use some of our newly gained college wisdom and bring the grill INSIDE.

The next morning when I awoke, I was met with a HUGE MESS in the kitchen and living room. True to my normal "mom-like" teenage self, I started cleaning up while everyone else was still racked out. At some point, I decided to take the bags of barbecue chicken remains (half raw, as I recall) out to the dumpster, which was probably about 150 feet from the front door of our condo.

While at the dumpster, I realized that there were some big cardboard boxes that would be perfect for flattening out and sledding on! Hey, remember we were BROKE COLLEGE STUDENTS. Our entertainment needed to be cheap!

So, there I was, alone in the closed-down ski resort's condominium parking lot in a remote town in Colorado, probably in my PJs, digging through a random dumpster while the sun was just coming up when ... a big white van drove up next to me.

The driver rolled his window down and said, "What are you looking for?" I remember laughing nervously and telling him my "cardboard boxes as sleds" theory, and then he proceeded to very nicely tell me that he lived "right up the way" and he'd be happy to lend us sleds to use while we were visiting. I, of course, told him "thank you," and he told me he could even run me up to his place real quick to get them.

Now, I know that every single one of you reading this is thinking, "Surely you didn't get IN THE VAN with him??"

In my defense, I do think I TRIED to say no, that I would just wait and come with my boyfriend later to get them, but he was pretty insistent that I go with him right then, and I didn't want to be rude.

When my eyes cracked open from my drunken stupor, I knew that if I didn't get water in me by the gallon, I would surely die. I stumbled downstairs to the kitchen, trying to figure out who had caused the massive barbecue explosion in the living room, and finally made it to the sink.

After funneling down as much water from the sink as I possibly could, I happened to glance out the now barbecue sauce-streaked window, only to see Susie climbing into a scary, white, serial-killerish VAN!

I splash water on my eyes, grab a paper towel and wipe the window, because, surely, I'm not seeing what I think I'm seeing???

Blinking furiously, I realize that my girlfriend is, indeed, climbing into said scary white van!! I race to the door, hung over and confused, and yell, "Suz!! What are you doing?"

"I'm GOING TO GET A SLED!"

What did she just say??? Did she say she's going to get a sled??

I yell again, this time with way more intensity,

"SUSIE, GET OUT OF THAT VAN!"

To which she yells back, all smiley and sing-songy, "It's FINE! I AM GOING TO GET A SLED!!"

At this point, I start making my way, boxer-clad and barefoot, through the snow towards the van and give her one last, "SUSIEEEEEEEE!!!! GET OUT OF THAT %*&@# VAN!!!!"

I remember looking over at Mr. Van Sled Guy and saying, "I think my boyfriend is really mad? I'm sorry. I guess I can't come with you to get the sled." He responded, "No worries, my cabin is just about 15 minutes up the mountain—you can't miss it—come by later and you can borrow them."

Needless to say, Chris wasn't happy with me when I got inside the condo and proceeded to let me know what a DUMB move it was to get in the van with a stranger. I defended my sled-saint and told Chris how nice he was. We got into a big fight and didn't speak for a bit, but true to both of our natures, we got over it pretty quickly and decided to go get the sleds.

Later I drove Susie up the mountain and guess what? We never saw one cabin.

Not. One. Cabin.

I'm pretty certain that if Chris had not awoken when he did (a miracle for sure!) and happened to look out the front window to see me climbing into that van, that I would've had my picture plastered on the sides of milk cartons for the next couple of decades and never have been heard from again.

So pretty much, I'm a freaking HERO.

So, when I tell you that I felt like I was betraying our close bond by accusing him of having a drinking problem that night, I'm not exaggerating. Plus, Chris was the "Man of the House," the "Provider," the "Protector" of the family. I knew that by me saying he had a "drinking problem," he would take it as me pretty much saying he was failing as a husband and father.

That's not what I thought, but I knew it was what he would think I meant.

I was actually shocked by his answer, as it was not the response I expected at all.

"I have been wondering for a while now when you would finally say something. The truth is, I have been making the effort to cut back and it's not working. I really don't know what to do and my inability to slow down is freaking me out."

This was the first time ever that, instead of being met with defensiveness or resistance to my questioning his drinking, I was met with submission and fear. Chris actually started crying as he admitted his inability to quit, and I think it was one of the only times in our 13 years together, at that point, that I had ever seen him cry.

I was scared. He was scared. And I was even more scared that he was scared. Neither of us had a clue as to what to do. Where do we go from here?

Wine. Wine is in the Bible. And it is supposed to be good for your heart. I can drink wine!

So, because we really didn't know WHAT to do, we concluded that if he quit drinking beer and instead drank wine, that would be a lot better. It was about that time that the heart healthy benefits of drinking red wine came out, and Chris was more than eager to provide me with *that* info.

I always got up earlier than Chris and, at the time, I was a pretty big clean freak. I started noticing these red spots throughout the kitchen and down the hallway … pretty much every morning. It took me a while to figure out what these spots were but it finally dawned on me … it was WINE.

So, Chris's new wine strategy might not be working out so great after all if he is sloshing wine down the hallway and throughout the house.

I was drinking wine with a funnel. Literally. Gallons of wine. I, had, in fact, stopped drinking beer and liquor but, certainly, the amount of wine I was drinking was overriding any health or Biblical justifications that I was creating. "Operation Wine" was failing.

CHAOS.

Chaos is a good word to describe how it felt a lot of the time, living with Chris and alcoholism at this point. He was really persuasive and really good at making me feel dumb for even questioning him if I thought he had been out drinking.

I'll never forget this one night though. He was still working at the mortgage company, and all day, he had told me that we would go get a Christmas tree with the kids as soon as he got off work. I think it was two weeks before Christmas, and we were literally the ONLY people who still didn't have a tree. And the kids didn't let me forget about it for even one moment.

So, it got dark and he wasn't home. I hadn't heard from him, and he wasn't answering his phone. The kids were upset, I was upset, and it definitely wasn't feeling like it was going to be a very merry Christmas after all.

Hours went by, and he finally showed up on the driveway with a tree in the back of his truck. The kids forgave him quickly and were just excited to get the tree out of the truck. As I was helping remove it from the back of his truck, I realized that I smelled alcohol. Very strongly.

I then maneuvered myself closer and realized he was so drunk he was slurring his words and swaying on the driveway. As I started to say something to him about his condition, he looked at me and said, "What? I can't hear you..." and then took off jogging down the street. Jogging. In his dress pants and dress shoes, in the pitch black and bitter cold night. The kids looked at me with big, questioning eyes and I just tried to act as normal as possible, and we got the tree inside.

After I got the kids tucked into bed, I just remember going into my closet, sliding down to the ground in a heap of despair, and sobbing and pleading to the Lord that He would "fix" my husband.

Chris eventually came into my closet and started trying to drunkenly explain himself, and I remember just screaming at him. Screaming that I couldn't take it anymore. Screaming that he shouldn't have been driving and he was failing me and the kids.

He yelled back at me and said to divorce him because he knew he was worthless.

We had a hard, fast rule that we would never speak of divorce so I was shocked when he said it ... but, what shocked me even more was that I found myself wondering if I actually would have to do that for the sake of my sanity and for the kids' safety.

The next day I went back and paid for that Christmas tree.

CHAPTER SEVEN

WHAT ABOUT GOD?

IF YOU'VE NEVER experienced living with someone with the disease of addiction, it's almost impossible to describe the rollercoaster of emotions you experience on a daily basis—hope, worry, relief, angst, happiness, sadness, loneliness, suspiciousness, and despair.

Addicts don't want to be addicts. They want to be NORMAL. Every day they promise that they will be better that day. And I think they truly mean it—or at least I know Chris meant it. It doesn't really matter if they "mean it" or not, though, as they are being controlled by the DISEASE. It has literally taken over their life and they are enslaved to it. They become really good at HIDING their habit. They become really good at lying and being sneaky.

When the addict is someone that you have trusted and loved for years, when the addict is your soul mate, you WANT to believe them. And you DO believe them up to a certain point … but that TRUST gets chipped away little by little over time until you have become a suspicious person that you don't even recognize.

I didn't want to lie. When I said I was going to do better, I meant it!

And I even bought what I was selling.

*   *   *

At that time, alcoholism was not something people talked about openly. Addiction was a dirty secret that was much better left hidden. It was not viewed as a "disease" — it was viewed as a WEAKNESS, a HUMAN DEFECT. I mean, it's a "CHOICE" after all, right??

I think there is still quite a bit of that in society today, but I do think we are seeing a movement of honesty and openness that is allowing people to seek help. But back then, I truly didn't feel I could talk to anyone. Only a few close friends had any clue as to what was going on, and they definitely didn't know the extent of the problem.

The burden I carried on my shoulders during that time is unlike anything I've ever experienced. Watching the one you love kill himself with alcohol, all while trying to maintain a good home environment for your kids and stay out of bankruptcy court, is an awful, terribly stressful existence. I will tell you, I started pleading to God like I never had before.

Maybe it would be Susie, Chris & God Against the World.

*   *   *

To just be totally transparent, there was not a whole lotta God talk in our relationship for quite some time, even though we were both brought up in Christian homes. We both accepted Christ as our personal Savior when we were quite young, and we both grew up attending great traditional churches (not together — we didn't meet until college, remember?).

My relationship with God took on a whole new meaning when I was 17 years old and almost died. There I was sitting in class one day, a normal high school student, healthy as a horse, when all of a sudden everything went fuzzy and dark. To give you some idea of what I mean, I wouldn't have been able to recognize my own mom if she had been standing a foot in front of me.

I was an athlete in school and just a normal healthy 17-year-old one minute, and then the next minute, practically blind.

I raised my hand, asking for the teacher to come to my desk and when she asked what I needed, I said, "I cannot see." She had just handed out a quiz and thought, because of my typical class clown antics, that I was just joking around to get out of the quiz. She said, "Sit down and take your quiz, McColl."

Ignoring her, I stumbled out of the classroom, thinking if I could just get to the nurse's office, she'd be able to help me get out whatever was in my eyes. With my hand against the wall, I was literally following the lockers based upon what I was feeling, and I somehow managed to find my way into the nurse's office.

Frantically, I explained to the nurse what was happening to my vision and she told me to calm down and that I was probably having some kind of allergic reaction because "people just don't lose their vision like that." She turned out the lights and, as she shut the door, said, "Close your eyes and rest for about 20 minutes, and then I'll be back to check on you."

This is when I learned that you can talk to God anytime, anywhere. "Lord, whatever is happening with my eyes, please make it stop! Help me see again."

Finally, the nurse came back in and asked if I was doing better. I told her no, and she called my parents to come and get me. My parents arrived, took me home, tucked me into bed, gave me some Robitussin and said that I'd be fine.

This is exactly what Chris does now when any of our kids are sick!!

However, I started having a terrible, excruciating headache—pain unlike anything I had ever felt before. I was moaning and crying, and my parents took me to the emergency room.

Once we arrived, all focus was on my eyes because of the newfound blindness I was experiencing. The doctor apparently stood me up in front of an eye chart (I couldn't see, so...) and asked me to cover my right eye and begin reading the letters on the chart with my left eye.

I told him, "I can't see the chart. I can't even see you!"

At this point, the nurse came in and took my blood pressure—now stuff was getting real. I remember her taking it three or four times saying, "This can't be right." My blood pressure was 274 over 173. I was literally having a stroke.

That's when panic set in, for me and the doctors and nurses around me. They quickly hooked me up to all sorts of machines and IVs and began pumping me full of medications, trying to bring down my blood pressure. A short while later, I heard the doctor say to my parents, "We're doing everything we can do but he's not getting any better—you should probably go in and say your goodbyes."

I remember lying on the table when, suddenly, my fingers involuntarily started pinching into each other and my arms started drawing into my body. I had no control over what was happening with my body. I remember my parents hovering over me, telling me how much they loved me.

The next thing I remember, I woke up and was in the ICU. Luckily, they were able to get my blood pressure under control and, thankfully, there was no apparent brain damage from the stroke I had just suffered.

The medical staff had no idea what had triggered my blood pressure to go so high and cause the stroke.

The crazy thing is, I remember feeling pretty normal again. I wasn't in pain and I could see! However, I was stuck in ICU with nurses everywhere, and they began to run a gazillion different tests. I remember one week, they decided I had a brain aneurysm. Another week, they thought it was something heart related. It was always something different.

There I lay, week after week, in the ICU but FEELING GOOD, just like I always had prior to my pre-blindness episode.

I can remember how every visitor coming into the ICU was the same. They'd peer nervously past my curtain as they made their way to visit their loved one who was also gravely ill. After a while, I got a bit tired of the peeping Toms, so my brother Tarpley and I decided to have some fun. As people were slowly walking towards my room, Tarpley would quietly announce they were coming, hide, and then I would start flopping uncontrollably all around to make it look like I was dying right as they peered around my curtain. The people would gasp and scurry on past as fast as they could go! My brother would pop up and we'd just roll with laughter. This was one way we passed the time.

Another favorite pastime was discussing medical things, you know, smart people stuff. How in the world did that hose sticking out from under my blanket get inserted into my privates??? Nobody ever thought to tell me that the big hose I was seeing was not the same size as the one actually inserted from the catheter into my private part internally.

After six weeks of being poked, prodded, scanned and tested, they finally identified that I had a rare tumor on my adrenal gland and it had actually wrapped around the bottom of my aorta.

Yep, this is where it gets real, people.

That tumor was called a pheochromocytoma, and the discovery of it led to a 13½-hour surgery where they cut me open from the top of my belly button to the top of my sternum. In the middle of the surgery, they actually had to flip me over onto my stomach and cut me open down my back, as well, because the tumor had spread so extensively throughout my chest cavity. They even had to remove two ribs, as well.

Remember when Chris told me it would take at least a year for me to get pregnant and so we passed on the birth control pills and bought bushes instead? Well, he used the rib removal from this surgery as a possible reason he wouldn't even be able to father kids at all.

Great news: if you are missing a rib or two, you can still have babies!!

Did I mention we were young and dumb when we got married?

They were able to remove the tumor, and I remember the doctors being excited over the discovery of such a rare tumor. They actually flew it to a major medical convention filled with physicians from all around the world to remind them to stay on the lookout for this rare and deadly tumor.

So, God had, in fact, brought my sight back, which was what I had begged him for. It was at that moment, after spending about three months in the hospital, as I walked out of the hospital, that I realized there are no guarantees for tomorrow.

This would change my outlook on life completely.

Three things I learned through this process:

1. I wasn't invincible,

2. There is no guarantee for tomorrow, and

3. God was real.

Not only was God real, but He had just saved me.

*   *   *

So with Chris's history, you'd think God would've been at the forefront of our relationship, right? Well … we were 18 and 20 and in love.

My parents were going through a divorce at the time that Chris and I started dating, so they had quit going to church, and that seemed to have put me in a non-churchy state of mind. Plus, I had gone to a private Christian school that was very strict and made me feel weekly that I should raise my hand and get saved all over again in chapel. Picture the whole "fire and brimstone" deal. I think I started associating being a Christian with feeling perpetually guilty.

We did get married in a church by Chris's family pastor, and we even attended that church for some time, until that pastor moved to a different state. Then, we really didn't attend church for a while. We were far too busy being in love with each other to have a whole lotta leftover time for God. And then, as we started having children, we were far too in love with *them* to have a whole lotta leftover time for God. We did start going to church because we knew it would be good for the kids, and it did become semi-important—right behind baseball, of course.

> Our kids were not just "playing" baseball. They were "in training" for the major leagues!!

But God.

God never gives up on us! God was there for us when we were too busy for Him. He waited patiently for us to turn back to Him.

And turn back to Him I did.

I remember praying fervently that He would help us figure out what to do and the steps to take to help Chris. I can remember feeling a comfort and knowing it could only be coming from my Heavenly Father. I dove into the Bible and started doing Bible studies. I remember learning a very simple prayer at that point that I started saying every day upon waking: "Lord, if nothing else, help me to grow closer to you today." And you know what? He answered that prayer during one of the hardest times of my life.

I, too, began diving into the bottle. I mean, Bible. I was doing research on exactly how Jesus was turning water into wine.

More on God's faithfulness later.

CHAPTER EIGHT

WE HAVE A RUNNER!

AFTER "OPERATION WINE" failed, things really went from bad to worse quickly. I had gone back to drinking beer and liquor, and I was starting to experience some pretty serious health issues that I was working hard to hide from Susie and the kids. One of those issues was vomiting. I was puking nonstop. And this is a big problem when you are trying to keep your alcohol down.

I can remember driving down the road and having to pull over behind some convenience store to lean outside my car and do a secret, sneaky puke.

This wasn't a one-time occurrence. This was happening all the time. I was puking so violently that yellow, nasty-tasting stuff was coming out. This was not your average puking—something was definitely, really wrong.

Body tremors and sleeplessness also started about this time. I would lie awake in fear and concern over what was going on with my body. I also was excessively irritable which, as you can imagine, did not go over so well at home with the family.

I had heard all the horror stories of alcohol withdrawal symptoms, and I had no desire to experience those. However, the only thing that seemed to alleviate all of my weird symptoms was ... you guessed it, drinking.

Not even just drinking. Drinking **MORE**.

I knew Chris was throwing up some, but he certainly didn't tell me to what extent. Did I mention that I was really busy with four young kids? Did I also mention that I am a professional avoider of conflict and negativity? I was only seeing what I chose to see, and honestly, I think I was coping the best I could at the time.

Plus, I had taken on the new role as "detective" of the McColl household. I would count the number of beer cans in the garage refrigerator, record them and compare them again the next morning. This way I would know how many cans of beer Chris was ACTUALLY drinking, not just what he told me.

Our older two boys actually got in on this detective work with me and would report to me if they saw Chris drinking when I wasn't around.

So, Susie started counting my beer cans. What this taught me was that I had to start hiding beer cans in a cooler under the ping pong table in the garage. I would take ONE can out of the fridge for every four or five I took out of the cooler.

This way, when she checked the beer stock in the fridge the next day, only two or three would be gone when in reality I had downed about 15.

Eventually I found the stocked cooler.

At this point, I knew I had to get some help. A buddy of mine sent me to his doctor and said he would be able to help me.

When I showed up to the doctor, I complained about the anxiety I was experiencing, but I blamed it on my job, money issues, and just general life stress. I left out the levels of alcohol I was actually consuming.

I honestly just wanted Dr. Fixit to tell me that the yellow nasty stuff I was throwing up all the time didn't mean I was about to die.

I left there with a handful of prescriptions for sleep and anxiety. From the doctor's perspective, all he heard was, "I'm not sleeping, I have a lot of anxiety, and I drink a little." So, he did his job and gave me some stuff to help.

I was so relieved that Chris had FINALLY gone to the doctor to get help. Things weren't really so great on the home front. He was gone a lot, but when he was home, he was either lying on the couch or in his recliner, not feeling good. I knew that some of it was from his drinking, but he also, once again, had me fooled that he had really cut back.

However, he had really began complaining about some major anxiety issues, so it was hard for me to get "mad" at him as I didn't want to further his stress.

But … I was becoming bitter that a lot of the load of taking care of the kids was resting squarely on my shoulders, and he was definitely not pulling his weight. So, I really hoped that the meds his doctor had just given him would help him function better and therefore help me out more.

* * *

Here's a fun fact: Mixing Xanax, Ambien and alcohol basically puts you into some kind of deep coma.

*   *   *

One day I was painting our bedroom. It was kind of a dark green color, and I was having to paint one coat of Kilz before I even got to the new color. I was doing the ceiling and all.

I can remember being on top of the ladder, straining to get around the ceiling fan and being so angry that Chris wasn't helping me. Not only was he not helping me, he hadn't even OFFERED to help me. Now, I could get a little crazy when I started one of my projects and didn't usually need or ask for help, but this bedroom painting project was a pretty tough job for one person.

I took a break to go find him to let him know what I thought of him not helping, but when I found him in the garage, I knew something was really wrong. He was lying on the floor of the garage and he looked really disoriented.

"Honey, what happened? Are you okay?" I asked him, my anger turning to concern immediately.

"I don't really know what happened ... I just ended up here like this. I think I might have had some weird seizure or something ..."

Well that did it. Obviously, THIS is a BIG problem.

I called his brother, and he agreed to meet us at the emergency room at our local hospital. I made arrangements for the kids, and off we went. On our way there, I was questioning him about the "event," but he was very disoriented and not really able to give me any coherent information.

Once we were in the ER, they immediately recognized that he was severely dehydrated and proceeded to give him two bags of IV fluids. In a shocking turn of events, he actually came clean about his drinking problem with the nurse attending him. She sent in a social worker who gave us information about detox centers.

Many of the options were crazy expensive, so they were immediately checked off the list because we really had NO money to spare at the time. Due to Chris's escalating drinking, he had changed jobs several times, which always left us "behind" and trying to catch up, just adding to his (and my) already high levels of stress.

Not only were these treatment centers extremely expensive, they were also extremely FULL. That left us basically with only one choice, a hospital downtown that offered a detox program followed by an inpatient rehabilitation program.

Now, you would think being in the ER and publicly discussing your hubby's drinking problem would be a somber event, right? Well, not when you are with Chris and his brother, Tarp. They deal with everything with HUMOR, and that day was no different. They had that nurse laughing her head off.

> My brother and I were fascinated by the IV bags and we even asked the nurse, "Can we put ANYTHING in these? So, it goes STRAIGHT into your system, huh? Can I get one of these to go? But, seriously, I don't have a problem..."

I remember laughing, but more than that, I remember feeling very RELIEVED that other people now knew about Chris's issue and we could finally get some real help.

So, the social worker set me up to go to a different hospital for a detox and rehab "program." The way they described it didn't sound too bad.

We got home and I started packing my bag. Susie was being annoyingly chipper, like we were going to be sitting around a fire, cooking s'mores, and I was freaking out because it was going to be really difficult to **NOT** drink, no matter what the environment.

Because, hey, let's call it what it was ... I was going to "cocktail camp."

*   *   *

In order for you guys to understand the significance of him agreeing to go to any hospital-type place, we need to revisit the three-month stay when he almost died at age 17. Have you heard of "White Coat Fever?" Well, I can tell you ... it's REAL. Chris had barely gone to the doctor for a check-up the entire time I had known him because he would immediately have anxiety and his blood pressure would go through the roof. Then he would have to explain his whole health history, so it was just a really stressful event for him altogether.

I couldn't believe he had actually agreed to go to a HOSPITAL for alcohol treatment. I knew at that point that this was not just a "serious" situation. This was truly a life or death situation.

We arrived downtown to the hospital with the program I'd be attending, and my anxiety was off the charts. I had a full-blown panic attack happening.

If you are lucky enough to have never experienced one, let me just tell you that it's like being trapped in a locked telephone booth with a tiger, and the feeling that you have to get out, no matter what, or you are going to die.

We went inside to the counter, and they gave us paperwork to fill out. As she began to explain how the program would work, I started looking around the waiting room, and it was packed full of people.

We go to sit down, and Susie starts filling out the paperwork. I tell her that I need to go outside and get some air. This turned into a death sprint to the convenience store I had seen down the road to buy my "medication" in the form of a Keystone Light tallboy to try to numb the full-blown panic attack I was experiencing.

I couldn't believe it. It was finally our turn to see the lady who would get him checked in, and I. COULD. NOT. FIND. HIM.

He told me he was going to get some air, but he was nowhere to be found.

I called him over and over, and he wouldn't answer his phone.

I let the lady know that I had a slight problem in that I couldn't find my husband, and she let me know that they only had one bed left and they wouldn't be holding it for long as they had an ever-growing waiting list.

I finally went back into the hospital, where I found a really frustrated Susie telling me that I was about to lose my spot. I was rejoicing on the inside, but on the outside, I probably acted disappointed.

They sent us down a hall, and at the end of the hall there was a metal door with a small glass window. There's no one there, so we peer through the window.

What I saw inside stopped me dead in my tracks.

I could see vacant-eyed patients milling around, smoking and wearing some kind of white robe thingies while talking to themselves.

And I'm pretty sure everyone in there had a cork on their fork.

I think those robes were actually straitjackets.

"I'm obviously NOT going in THERE."

"Chris! Yes, you are! You agreed, and we filled out all the paperwork. It's only 30 days! And it's the only option we can afford."

"30 DAYS!!! I thought you said 3 DAYS!!! I can't survive in there 3 minutes!!! What are you going to do? Throw me in there, yell 'Alcoholic' and slam the door behind you???? I'm NOT going in there!!"

I wanted to argue further with him because I was too scared to take him back home in the same condition, but then we both just stood there peering through the glass window for a few more moments and I said, "Okay, let's go home." As much as I wanted to get him help, this definitely didn't look like the right atmosphere.

It was at this moment that I realized just how difficult it is to get help for people facing addiction. I don't know if I've ever felt so hopeless or defeated as I did in that moment.

We walked back downstairs and told the lady that I was not staying. We asked her if she had any other advice or options, and she actually gave us the phone number of a psychiatrist that would sometimes do detox on an outpatient basis.

"Now THIS is what I'm talking about!!" I thought. 'Outpatient' became my new favorite word. Why hadn't they told us about this miraculous outpatient (aka stay-at-home) program, before now???

*   *   *

So, there we were, back home and him back on the couch. I truly remember feeling like the man I loved, the father of my children, my soul-mate, was basically just dying on the couch, and I could do nothing to help him. I remember going for a walk in the neighborhood, taking a deep breath and calling my momma to tell her what was going on.

It's not exactly an "easy" topic of conversation to tell your family that your husband is dying from alcoholism and your lives are falling apart. I know she consoled me that day but, even more, she said something to me that day that I will never forget. She said, "Susie, I am so proud of the wife and mother that you have become. You are strong and they are lucky to have you." Listen, I NEEDED someone to be proud of me. I needed someone to tell me that I was going to be okay. This was such a life lesson for me - if you are proud of someone you love, TELL THEM. You never know how much your words of encouragement might empower them. I also remember hanging up the phone with my mom and crying out to the Lord, "Please help us, God. Please help us find a way for him to get better. I don't know what to do here, Lord.

I need you." I might be a pretty strong person but for this I needed God's strength!

I called the psychiatrist the very next morning, and he hesitantly agreed to see us. I say hesitantly because I think he was incredibly busy with a full patient load and also because I don't think outpatient detox is the most ideal solution. Nevertheless, he agreed, told me it would be $250 (which was a huge relief, although even that was a lot to us at that time), and we were on our way.

When we rolled up on this place, it looked like some kind of hippie commune, not what I had imagined a psychiatrist's office would look like. But, hey, I was up for anything as long as it was on the "stay-at-home" program.

The psychiatrist, who fit the mold of the hippie commune leader, sat me down on the couch and asked me some probing questions. He told me there were probably some underlying issues causing the drinking, and at some point, we should explore those things. He handed me some "natural" pills, wrote me a prescription for lithium and said, "You should probably stop drinking. It's only going to get worse."

I high five'd him, thanked him for the stuff, walked out into the waiting room, and told Susie, "I'm cured!"

Looking back, I don't think she laughed.

So my at-home detox program was actually a descending dosage of lithium. This was the first time I had ever heard of lithium, but apparently it, like Xanax or Valium (all part of the benzodiazepines class of drugs), touches the same nerve receptors as alcohol, and it would help my body safely detox from the alcohol in my body.

With the amount of alcohol I had been consuming, apparently you can't just quit cold turkey without the possibility of having a heart attack or seizure. I guess that might explain what I had experienced in the garage that day prior to us making the first trip to the ER and getting help.

As we were driving home from the psychiatrist's office that day, I remember feeling cautiously optimistic that *maybe* this would work. Maybe Chris could finally get all of the alcohol out of his system and just be back to CHRIS! Back to the guy that was my best friend, my confidante, my soul mate. Back to the fun dad that liked to play with the kids outside. Back to the Chris that loved to make us all laugh and who we all knew so well and loved.

CHAPTER NINE

SECRETS, SECRETS, SECRETS

SOBER LIFE WAS working! Except for when I was drinking ... But, wait, I'm getting ahead of myself. Let me back up a minute.

I did actually get completely SOBER, and I couldn't believe that I was doing it and how great I felt.

There was no "program"—I wasn't attending AA meetings or anything like that. I was simply doing the "Chris-stay-home-and-don't-drink" program.

I had to pull back from some of my relationships that had always revolved around drinking. The same went for many activities that also revolved around drinking. Fishing and drinking, golfing and drinking, drinking and drinking. You get the picture.

One of the hardest parts of my newfound sobriety was figuring out WHAT exactly I could do WITHOUT drinking.

I think anyone that has lived with an alcoholic would tell you that it's difficult to trust for a while once said alcoholic "gets sober." Especially if you read all the statistics about relapse. I think I felt I had to be vigilant in my "sobriety watch" for Chris to STAY sober—which is funny, now that I look back, that I thought I had that kind of control.

However, being that I just happen to be one of the most trusting individuals on the planet (remember the "Going to Get a Sled" story?), I did start trusting him more and happily giving up my detective ways. The more time that went by and the more I saw him thriving and healthy again, the more comfortable I became.

> I think I made it completely sober about a solid year. At first, it was fairly easy because my focus and attention was entirely on me **NOT** drinking. I didn't have any history of success before this, so I just focused on the day-to-day. I wasn't going to drink. Period. I was very transparent with Susie, and that helped keep me accountable.

One thing, though, that always bothered me was his secrecy about getting sober. He did not want to discuss it with anyone, and he definitely didn't want ME to discuss it. I am a very open book and probably tell way too many details of my life, though, so I just thought it was a difference in our personalities.

> If I told people I was an alcoholic in recovery, then they would KNOW that if I was drinking, I shouldn't be! Of course, I didn't want to tell people.

> Going into the second year of sobriety, I slowly began letting my guard down. Having a glass of wine was fine because I had made it a year, after all. That was proof that I was capable of only drinking when I wanted to drink, right? Having a couple of beers on the golf course with my brother was no big deal, right?? I wasn't out getting wasted or excessively drinking, I was just doing what all guys do to relax. Doesn't a guy deserve to relax??

This, of course, was happening in the shadows, without Susie knowing because she was still on the "sober-all-the-time" program and I was on the "sober-most-of-the-time" program.

There were times in that second year that I would actually start to worry he was drinking again. I always hated to question him, though, because he would get his feelings hurt that I would question his sobriety. But sometimes there was just something "off" about him and I knew it. He was very, very good at convincing me that I was being a bit crazy, though, and I would usually just back down.

So in year two of my newfound "sobriety," I began to become an increasingly sneaky drinking professional. This meant that I got really good at hiding any consumption I might have had through various tactics that only a true, full-blown alcoholic can appreciate.

Let's chat about some of these methods so you can understand the level of professionalism I attained:

Have you ever heard of O'Doul's? It's a brand of non-alcoholic beer. I started buying these with good intentions of actually drinking them, but pretty quickly, they became nothing more than mouthwash. If I was drinking O'Doul's, which Susie was totally okay with, it was license to drink as much real beer as I wanted to behind the scenes because if I smelled like it, it must be the O'Doul's.

Now you might think that's pretty smart, but that's amateur stuff—I raised the bar (pun intended).

I began pouring out the non-alcoholic beer and replacing it with REAL beer. I basically had my own bottling business in my garage. I'd be walking around holding my O'Doul's NON-alcoholic beer bottle filled with my fave brand, Coors Light.

Everyone was so proud of my commitment to my sobriety.

Oh yes, O'Doul's. I thought it was a true God-send for us at the time. Chris could drink it and feel like he wasn't missing out! I remember picking it up for him at the grocery store and thinking it sure was pricey but totally worth it. Obviously, I wasn't aware that he was actually watering our bushes outside the garage with it at home.

Here's another example. There wasn't enough teeth-brushing or mouth-washing (for the record, I wasn't drinking the mouthwash ... yet) that could go on. No matter what I drank, I could find a way to scrub it or cover it. Mints and gum were my best friends at all times.

Altoids. He ALWAYS had them in his pocket.

Did you know that if you pour a little bit of Gatorade out of the bottle and add vodka that it just looks like... Gatorade? I became one of the biggest Gatorade consumers on the planet in those days. So, what started out as "occasional drinking," barely interrupting my sobriety, started increasing in frequency. Golf tournaments, fishing tournaments, baseball tournaments, Father's Day, 4th of July, Labor Day—everybody drinks.

Now it's Tuesday and its nice outside.

Doesn't everybody drink? Except Susie?

Chris always wanted me to drink. He would always say, "Just because I can't drink and enjoy myself, doesn't mean you can't! It makes me feel bad that you don't drink on account of me." But the thing was, I had seen firsthand what alcohol could do to our family, and I had begun to LOATHE it. It was pretty much the devil in a bottle to me.

*　　*　　*

Now, here is when things started to slide downhill quickly. It was probably the beginning of year 3 of me being "sober" when I had excruciating dental pain—like somebody was hitting my tooth with a ball-peen hammer kind of pain. I called my dentist and reported the pain, and he called me in some pain meds and set up an appointment the following week.

Take special note of this day because this led to some of the deepest, darkest places I've ever been in my life.

Pain medication sure did help with the pain. But, more than that, it also enlightened me to the fact that they also mimicked having a few beers.

Up to this point, I had never, to my knowledge, taken pain meds, although I probably did that time when I almost died in high school. When I realized that I could pop one of these bad boys and get the same sensation of having four, five, or six beers—with absolutely NO EVIDENCE, no smell, no empty bottles, no having to have my own re-bottling company in the garage—I knew, without a doubt, that this was going to be a GAME CHANGER when it came to "Operation-Chris-Is-Kind-of-Sober."

Obviously, I know NOW that this sounds completely illogical, but it made complete and utter sense to me then!!

My tooth got fixed, but my desire to get these little magic pills did not. It was such a relief to ONLY have to worry about keeping my pills refilled and not have to constantly worry about hiding beer cans and my drinking from Susie.

*   *   *

At this time, our daughter had gotten very competitive in gymnastics and spent four hours four nights per week at a gym about 30 minutes from our house. (We were still in our crazy sports phase, obviously!)

She was also experiencing a lot of "gymnastics anxiety," so she would beg for me to stay with her ... all four hours. Which I did, although I can remember feeling very guilty for always being gone from home and the boys.

Chris knew how stressed Macy was at that time, so he wholeheartedly encouraged me to stay with her.

If Susie was gone at gymnastics in the evenings, I could take a magic pill or two and start "relaxing" a lot earlier.

I can remember coming home at about 9 p.m. and the boys would already be asleep. Chris would be in his recliner in front of the TV, either snoring or basically comatose. I just assumed it was because it was late, although the boys did start complaining to me that, "Dad makes us go to bed at like 7 p.m. when you aren't home!" Looking back, I feel silly that I didn't know what was going on.

I should have known.

Especially because we started having fights about him slurring his words and being so out of it.

But, you remember those pills for anxiety Dr. Fixit had given him? He blamed his actions on those. And ... he had ANXIETY and NEEDED them.

And I guess I bought it.

I think it was easier to buy that than to accept the truth.

*   *   *

Let me tell you about a day that changed everything. My brother had invited me to a golf tournament. I was pretty sure that I was going to experience more tooth pain that day, so I decided to take one, maybe two, of my pain pills.

I'll never forget—on about the third hole, it was the first time that I ever drank alcohol along with my magic pills.

Here I was, in a golf tourney, on a gorgeous day, drinking a "few beers" with my bro ... on top of taking my previously discussed magic pills.

Things ramped up so quickly that there was no stopping it. I was PLASTERED. The can't-stand-up-slurring-my-words kind of plastered. Since the golf tourney lasted several days, my lucky, alcoholic self had pre-planned staying at a hotel—so there would be no Susie or kids around to witness this stupor I was in.

Through this event, I learned that this combo of pain pills and alcohol was ... AWESOME. The more I consumed the magic pills mixed with alcohol, the more I craved.

My addictive personality was in love with a dangerous combination, setting the stage for a train wreck of ultimate proportions.

I remember that golf tournament well because I remember worrying whether he'd be strong enough to stay sober. I can vividly remember standing on the driveway in the dark, hugging him hard and asking, "Do you really have to stay in a hotel? I'll miss you!" Not that I wouldn't miss HIM, but I was actually just worried that I'd miss any signs of him DRINKING.

*   *   *

It turns out the dentist won't just keep refilling pain pills after you've had a root canal done. So, I became a bit "injury prone" at this point. Back and knee injuries all came with doctor visits and more pain pills.

For a guy that had White Coat Fever and had avoided doctor visits like the plague for years, I became quite the connoisseur of doctors in my hometown.

*   *   *

The throwing-up problem (that sent me to the hospital back before Getting Sober Attempt #1) had returned with a vengeance.

One day, I was at home and was feeling really whacky and sick. Something was off, seriously off. I didn't know what, and I certainly couldn't share with Susie all of my symptoms because I had been hiding so much about the pain pills and alcohol.

But I knew that I needed to get help.

I remember Chris being "sick" again. This had started happening more and more frequently. Just about a week prior to this day, he actually had missed my grandma's funeral because he was home puking and in bed. You'd think I would've suspected alcohol at this point, based on the first episode years earlier, but he always managed to convince me of other valid reasons he was sick.

Again, addicts become very good at covering up and making their loved ones feel silly for questioning them.

I called my brother and told him I was pretty bad off. He came over, scooped me up and took me to the hospital.

I told Susie that I didn't want her to come because she needed to stay home with the kids.

Once in the hospital, they started discussing my symptoms and doing all sorts of lab work. I quickly realized that they were starting to identify the hidden problem. They started asking me about alcohol consumption and any other meds I might be taking. For a lot of this, I was in a fog, but I know I was deliberately steering them in a wrong direction because I was so fearful Susie would show up and they'd tell her what was going on.

I can remember telling her that I was fine, that they were just running tests and she was better off at home with kids.

I did show up to the hospital, and the doctor—a really nice woman that I learned went to our church, actually—kept trying to tell me about his lab work, but Chris kept butting in.

I did not want that doctor to tell her what was really going on!!

And what was really going on was that my daily cocktail of alcohol and pain meds was taking a big toll on my body. I was very dehydrated and deficient in all sorts of necessary vitamins and nutrients. They were pumping me with a vitamin-infused IV.

I remember this nurse coming into my room, saying, "You're going to be okay," in a way that meant I really might not be okay.

They finally gave Chris an official diagnosis of "pancreatitis." Apparently, pancreatitis is caused by two things—excessive alcohol usage or a bad gallbladder. To tell you just how freaking clueless I was, or just how much we can talk ourselves into believing what we WANT to believe, I went with the bad gallbladder and actually remember telling my brother and dad that.

I mean, we all googled the cause of pancreatitis and we all read that the #1 cause was excessive drinking. Dang Google.

I WANTED it to be his gallbladder.

Please, dear Lord, let his bad gallbladder be the sole reason for all of his recent horrible health issues.

I did NOT want it to be drinking, AGAIN. He was sober, after all.

My freaking gallbladder. Of course, it's my stupid gallbladder. What does a gallbladder even do? I'm clearly going to have to get my gallbladder out.

Wait, surely, they give you pain pills after they take out your gallbladder?? It is an organ and it is surgery, after all?

This got me thinking ... what other unnecessary body parts could I have removed in the future to get more happy pills? Do I even really need my left arm?

Chris did, in fact, get his gallbladder out shortly after this hospital stay. I was so surprised that he actually went through with it because this was the same guy that had avoided the doctor at all costs the entire time I had known him. His gallbladder must really be causing him pain.

He was super insistent that we drive straight from the hospital to the pharmacy to get his pain pills filled. The crazy thing was, his driver's license had expired unbeknownst to him, so the pharmacy wouldn't fill the prescription. We actually drove from the pharmacy to the tag agency to get his new license, picture and all.

Oh, you gotta' see this picture. Me, hours out of the hospital after surgery, and I'm now stamped for the next five years with a picture that could well have been my prison mugshot.

But I got my pain pills.

I remember feeling so relieved, thinking now that we got his gallbladder taken care of, surely, he'll get back on the path to good health.

CHAPTER TEN

HOUSTON, WE HAVE A "PROBLEM"

SHOCKINGLY, OR MAYBE not so shockingly, I ran out of pain pills pretty quickly after my gallbladder surgery. I called the doctor and told them I was in incredible amounts of pain, and they continued to fill my prescription … for a while.

The thing with pain pills is that you start building up a tolerance for them, so the amount you need steadily increases. I was running out way faster than I should be running out. These pills—mixed with alcohol, of course—were proving to be a NECESSITY.

My gallbladder doctor finally cut me off, so I had to start doctor shopping again in order to keep the supply flowing.

I remember one day, after leaving another doctor appointment where I claimed to have "lost" my pain pills, the thought occurred to me that I was definitely TRAPPED.

Let me explain what I mean by "trapped." My only concern in LIFE at this point was how to acquire more meds and more alcohol—all while trying to keep it secret from Susie, the kids and anyone else I knew at the time.

So, he had come through the gall bladder surgery, and I was optimistic that he would finally be better. Maybe he would finally be back to the Chris that helped me with the kids and homework, the Chris that took the boys to their baseball games, the Chris that mowed the yard and helped with chores around the house ...

However, that didn't really happen. He didn't bounce back, and he blamed it all on severe pain from the surgery. I was a bit confused as I read enough about gallbladder surgeries to know they weren't that crazy painful of a surgery. When I would suggest this to Chris, however, he would get very defensive and make me feel horrible for suggesting he was a wimp. Many, many fights happened over this and I just got TIRED of all the fighting, so I would basically keep my mouth shut.

*   *   *

At this point, I had graduated from washing my pain pills down with beer to vodka. I came up with some pretty awesome concoctions for my vodka, too. My favorite such concoction was filling a Gatorade bottle 3/4 of the way up with vodka and then 1/4 with Gatorade, and then I would actually stash these throughout the house. One of my best stash places was in the spare tire compartment underneath the trunk of my car.

Oh, don't get me wrong, I still loved beer, but Susie had some uncanny smelling sense and could always detect beer on me. I HAD to switch to vodka to continue my sneakiness.

A huge thank-you to the kind soul that let me know vodka can't be smelled on you.

Actually, that's not true. If you drink ENOUGH vodka, the smell actually starts seeping out through your pores. I knew Chris had a weird odor. It just took me a while to figure out it was vodka.

> On a daily and nightly basis, I would "wake up" (even though I really barely slept—insomnia is a side effect of alcohol withdrawal) and go out into the garage to chug my vodka concoctions. I was constantly faking illnesses where I would spend 24 to 48 hours in bed at a time, but I was actually just pain pilling and drinking.

> And I truly was "sick," alright.

Ugh. These are hard memories to make myself relive. I can remember being up by 6 a.m., doing my Bible study, getting all four kids clothed, fed and breakfasted, making their lunches, and getting them all off to school.

I'd finally get home from taking them—four kids in three different schools at this time—and he'd still be in BED. Hours after I had gotten up.

It was so irritating, and I was growing more and more bitter that he was basically doing NOTHING to help me. He was always "sick." As I mentioned earlier, I started every day by praying, "Lord, if nothing else, help me to grow closer to You today."

I also, at this point, had caught Chris drinking again and KNEW that he was having issues. I didn't know to what extent and I didn't know about the pain pills, but many evenings he would slur his speech and not make much sense. He would blame his "anxiety pills" that he convinced me he HAD to have, and he would promise to call the doctor and get them changed.

*   *   *

What I truly remember about this particular time in our lives is how HOPELESS I felt. Since Chris was always sick, he was basically bouncing between jobs. We were dead broke, our house was even in foreclosure and I couldn't get a job that would pay me enough to pay for the daycare the kids would require.

Luckily, my dad and brother had graciously given me a job of packing up my grandparent's farmhouse of 50 years. It was on some family land that was being developed. I would take the kids to school and then drive 30 minutes to the property to work, many days leaving Chris at home "sick" and in bed.

My mom, dad and brother were some of only a handful of people that had known about Chris's drinking problem the first go around, but up to this point, I had kept Chris's relapse from them. I didn't want my family to think badly of him, to think badly of US.

Because, I promise you, addiction is a FAMILY disease with a big ol' heaping side effect of SHAME.

I remember one day I was at the farm house in the living room, packing up my Grammy's glass mementos, and the song, "Never Let Go," by David Crowder, a Christian artist, came on the radio. The lyrics basically say that, no matter what troubles you are going through, God is there for you. That God is "ever faithful, ever true," that His love is perfect and He will "never let go."

Every word of that song pierced my soul. I remember all the strength, that I was trying so hard to be full of, leaving my body as I collapsed, sobbing, onto some stairs near me.

As dark as our current situation was, the Lord was reminding me that He was there for me. His PERFECT love was the same for me, and for Chris, in the good times and the bad. We were HIS and He wouldn't abandon us.

I believe the Lord was specifically speaking to me through that song that day and if that weirds you out, that's okay. To this point in my life, I have never actually audibly heard the Lord's voice, but I do believe the Lord finds ways of speaking to us all the time—through songs, actual signs, friends and family, church messages, a well-timed verse or passage in the Bible—it's just a matter of if we are open to hearing from Him.

At this point, I just truly did not know what to do. I knew that Chris needed help, but I didn't know who to turn to and I didn't know how we would possibly even pay for any treatment we could get him. My dad had already been incredibly generous, helping us out financially over and over again, so I didn't want to ask him. I started calling treatment places. Most of them didn't have openings, and if they did, they didn't take insurance and might as well have cost a million dollars based upon how much money we had at that point.

I felt, just as the song I listened to that day says, that the "water" was rising over my head and that my "hope had flown." Every time I hear that song to this day, I get all teary because it brings back allllll the emotions of that day. But, as weird as it sounds, I wouldn't take a minute of that day back because I KNEW the Lord was with me that day.

I also credit this lonely, hopeless time as the time that brought me fully back to the Lord. I talked with Him more than I ever had before, and I would literally beg to feel His comforting arms around me. I prayed that He would give me the wisdom to know when Chris was drinking and when he was lying to me, something that was happening more and more. He answered this prayer, too.

*   *   *

One day, I was pulling out of the baseball field parking lot and happened to shine my lights right on Chris's truck. He was still inside the ballpark watching one of our older boys play in a high school game, and I was leaving early to get our younger two kiddos in bed.

Anyways, my lights happened to shine right on his truck, and I caught a glimpse of something underneath his truck. I don't know how to explain this, but I knew that I knew that I knew that I was going to find alcohol under his truck.

Sure enough, I pulled next to his truck, got out of my car, fished out a sack from under the middle of his truck and it had two Keystone Light tallboy EMPTY cans in it. God was answering my prayers and giving me the wisdom and guidance I had asked for.

Later that night when he got home, I confronted Chris about the sack of beer cans, which I, of course, held up like a lawyer presenting evidence in a court case. I cannot truly remember his response, but I know he was genuinely shocked that I had found the sack. We ended up in a HUGE blow-up fight, with him storming out of the house and off into the night.

I still don't know how she found that sack! The Lord was obviously cramping my sneaky drinking game!!! Susie's newfound direct line to God was obviously going to create some major problems!

All of this crazy chaos finally reached full momentum when Tanner, our oldest son, was going to play in a high school baseball tourney on a spring break trip in Florida. At home, it was pretty much Susie VS. Me and My Drinking, so I hatched a plan that involved me going to Florida by myself while Susie stayed home with the other kids and "saved us the money we couldn't afford to spend" ... or so that's how I justified it to her.

The true reason I wanted to go alone is because it would allow me to drink and take my happy pills as much as I wanted to with no "Susie Private Eye" watching my every move.

I dropped this plan so quickly that I was basically already on the road to Florida when I let Susie in on it.

So began my 847-mile trek across the country when I shouldn't have even have been driving across the street from my house. The only way I'm writing about this trip right now is that the Lord protected me from myself. That's the only logical answer on how I'm still alive.

I still vividly remember talking to Chris on the phone as he was leaving town for this trip. I was at a baseball tournament with our youngest son, Maddox, and I couldn't even concentrate on the game because I was pretty sure it was a really, really bad idea for Chris to be driving anywhere, let alone by himself, across the country.

But he told me his plan and then hung up. He wouldn't answer as I called him back over and over again.

Once again, I felt a deep despondency because I had to shoulder the burden of this fear alone. It wasn't like I could just walk over to the other smiling, cheering parents sitting on the bleachers, eagerly hoping for hits, catches and outs, and say, "Does anyone know what I should do about my husband being most likely hammered while driving across the country and not answering his cell phone?" I mean, that kinda would've put a damper on the game for everyone, don't ya think?

This trip was basically a liquor store tour from Oklahoma City to Florida. I was sleeping in my car in strange places because, of course, when you are broke and on the road, you have to save all your money for your alcohol. Logical, right?

I continued to call him over and over that afternoon and night, only getting his voicemail. I finally got on my computer that night, lying in bed worried sick, and used our cell phone carrier's new "Family Where" service to track his phone. We had recently gotten this service to be able to track our oldest two boys (16 and 17 years old at the time). I didn't, however, imagine that I'd be using it to track Chris. But, sure enough, I could see Chris's phone on a map and it looked like he was parked next to a lake. At that point, I honestly worried whether he was even alive.

There was no lake. The problem was Susie knew my current state of mind and she assumed I was oblivious to the lake right in front of me, even though it was actually a wheat field.

Oh my gosh ... maybe that wasn't a wheat field. Maybe it WAS a lake.

The disease of addiction is a lonely road. The addict isolates himself. The spouse of the addict doesn't feel like they can confide in anyone, and so they isolate themselves. And then we put on a brave face and act like everything is "fine" to the world ... when really, everything is falling apart and you are just trying to survive.

CHAPTER ELEVEN

LOST AND FOUND

BY THE GRACE of God, I made it to Florida.

The fact that I did not wreck, kill other people or myself, is truly miraculous. Once I got there, I remember being really lost and not sure where the baseball tournament was at or even where all of the baseball team was, including my son.

Somehow, some way, I finally found the team parents who I had always enjoyed having a good time with. However, it became apparent pretty quickly, through their responses to me, that in no way, shape or form they thought I should be driving or even walking—which was proven to be the truth as I rolled my ankle, fell to the ground and could not get myself up.

Some of my longtime friends got me to my feet, obviously aware that I was completely incapacitated. They asked me to call someone for help because, clearly, I was not capable of helping myself. I, of course, denied needing help or the offer to call anyone and so they basically put me to bed.

Based on some texts I got from some of the other baseball parents, I knew that Chris had finally arrived in Florida for the tournament. However, he wasn't answering his phone, which had me deeply concerned. Eventually I got a picture of what must be going on there, as one of the moms suggested in a text that she knew of a church ministry that might be able to help Chris get control of his drinking.

That text sent my worry into a new stratosphere. I was at home and helpless to do anything. The only thing I could do was pray. And boy did I pray. Oh, and to top it off, it was spring break for our kiddos and they were making me feel guilty for not taking them to do anything fun. Here my husband was virtually lost and doing who knows what in Florida, and I had to put on the "fun charade" so that my kids had an appropriately fun Spring Break. Motherhood does not stop in times of emergency.

I woke up the next morning in virtually the same state I had gone to bed a few hours earlier, still basically inebriated. I remember thinking to myself, "I have to get out of here before I further embarrass Tanner in front of his team."

I started to make my way back to my car where I was promptly greeted by some of my friends, telling me in no way they could let me drive. At this point, they pretty much forced me to call Susie.

That phone call from Chris was the worst phone call of my entire life. I don't even know how to describe how bad Chris sounded. He sounded lost, alone, scared, desperate ... He was saying things that weren't making much sense, so I knew his brain was not functioning fully. He was crying, and then I was crying.

I remember telling him that it would all be okay, that *he* would be okay. I told him that I loved him with all my heart and we would work through this together. I know that I was very worried he might even take his life. Don't forget, this was my soulmate, my best friend, the yin to my yang ... Chris & Susie Against the World.

I was terrified in that moment that I was about to lose him forever. I told him to just hang on a few minutes and that I was going to call his brother, Tarpley, because he would know what to do. That seemed to calm him down a bit, as Tarpley has always been an anchor for him, and I did just that. It took Tarpley, me, Chris's parents and that "Family Where" service, but we did manage to find him.

Here I was, a fully-grown man, waiting for my mommy and daddy to drive four hours from their house in Tuscaloosa, Alabama, to pick me up in Florida because I was "lost" and had no clue what to do.

My parents picked me up, found the "lost" key to my car that I had sworn was nowhere to be found (um, it was in my back pocket—super tricky of me!), and hauled me back to their couch in Tuscaloosa.

I really don't think my parents had any clue as to how bad off I actually was. There I was, literally sleeping on their couch for days trying to recover from whatever hell I had put myself through on the days prior ... but I was SICK. I was so sick that, as I started to feel the scary symptoms of withdrawal, it drove me to my parent's liquor cabinet to drink whatever I could get my hands on and then quickly put it back so they wouldn't know.

On about my third trip to the liquor cabinet, I realized that I'd drank so much of my dad's favorite liquor, that he'd definitely be able to tell. So, I took the bottle to the faucet and filled it up with water. Dad, if your favorite whiskey seemed a little watered down, sorry, that was me.

I was still a sneaky drinking professional.

*   *   *

I was at home in Oklahoma trying to figure out HOW to get Chris home. He was staying on his parents' couch and he was putting on a good show to me (via phone) that he was doing better. However, I couldn't and WOULDN'T forget that awful phone call with him a couple days prior and I knew that he needed help, real help. However, I couldn't DRIVE there because then we would have two cars there. Flying was really expensive, but that seemed to be my only option. I'm sure I found some credit card that had just enough room and booked my one-way ticket.

At this point, I still had not told anyone (other than Chris's family) what was going on, but the "life is good" facade was about to crumble as I needed some help.

The liquor from my parent's liquor cabinet was really not touching my withdrawal symptoms because I was out of pain pills. I was throwing up, having diarrhea, shaking all over, pacing around my parents' house nonstop, and trying to figure out: (a) was I going to die?, (b) if I didn't die, would Susie actually kill me?, or (c) could I possibly get my hands on some pain pills to make the fear of A and B go away?

I called one of my best friends, gave her a brief, teary version of what was going on, and asked if she could take care of my younger two kids. She graciously offered to do anything she could to help.

Next, I had to tell Carson. I was so dreading having to tell him what was going on, but I remember it like it was yesterday. I was out in the garage, sweeping the floor with a broom (because I clean and "do all the things" when I'm stressed), when Carson arrived with his girlfriend. I told him what was happening with his dad but started crying and couldn't really speak. He took the broom from me, set it aside, and hugged me so tight. He said he could drive me to the airport and take care of things at the house until I got home. I was in awe of how mature he was.

And I was thankful that I had someone to share my fears with. Hiding reality from everyone and holding all of your emotions in gets really, really tiring after a while.

*   *   *

On about the 4th day on my parent's couch, I convinced my dad he needed to take me to the hospital. That something was really wrong with me.

Now remember, Susie had been calling nonstop and in constant communication with my brother and my parents, but I'd purposefully been vague about my condition because I thought I could pull it together and she'd never have to know just how bad I was.

As we circled outside the hospital before we went in, my dad said, "You know you are going to be fine, right? You are not going to die." I don't think I fully believed him.

After a short questionnaire, the doctor realized that I had massive amounts of anxiety and sent me out the door with instructions to rest and a prescription for Valium. I had never had Valium before, but hey, the doctor was right! It was awesome and I felt so much better!

So much so that I called Susie and let her know the good news—I was fine! She disagreed and said I sounded "loopy," but I assured her I was fine.

He was completely loopy. I let him know that I had a one-way ticket and that I'd be there soon to get him and bring him home.

Oh my gosh, Susie was coming to get me. I needed somebody to hide me because SUSIE WAS COMING TO GET ME. We were broker than broke, and she was flying to "get" me—and when I say "get," I really mean "kill."

*   *   *

My parents drove me to the airport where I would be meeting Susie. Now, in case you think I'll be FLYING home with her, you'd be wrong. Remember I have my CAR ... I just can't drive it.

I'm about to experience a 10-hour lecture, scolding, beatdown of epic proportions, all the way home. Oh yeah, and I have no answers to the problems I'm experiencing.

So, let's sum this up real quick. I had driven to Florida (apparently) ... made a complete fool of myself in front of a whole baseball team of parents and kids ... I'd gotten lost, lost my keys in my back pocket and had to be picked up by my mommy and daddy ... and then, to make it even more fun, my wife had to FLY to pick me up and drive me and my car home. Yay.

There was a chance that the last part might not, in fact, have been true—there was a chance she was going to be driving me to a secluded area simply to put me out of my own misery.

I tried to hold it together on the plane because I felt perilously on the edge of tears. Plus, I knew I had to be strong for Chris when I got to him. I just remember thinking on the plane, "How did we get here? How is this our life right now?"

With my head down, staring at the ground, preparing for a severe verbal beating, I peered out of one eye and spied not an angry Susie like I had imagined, but, instead, this "Angel of Love" coming towards me with her arms wide open to embrace me. She squeezed me tight, kissed me and started telling me everything would be okay. She said, "We'll get through this. I'm just so happy you are alive."

We took off into the dark night without a clue as to what we were going to do, but I know both of us felt better just being together. We drove for a few hours and finally stopped at a hotel, drop dead exhausted.

With Susie's arms around me that night in that little hotel bed, I felt such a huge sense of relief. The lies, the deceit, the never-ending hamster wheel of darkness wasn't gone yet, but it was at least out in the light. I no longer felt alone. I still had no idea how I was going to get "fixed," but at least, for the first time in a long time, I felt a sense of **HOPE**.

* * *

The next morning when we went to get in Chris's car, he said to me, "I can drive." I just laughed at him and said, "Get in the passenger seat, buddy." It's an ongoing thing with us that he hates my driving and ALWAYS drives, but, on this particular day, he couldn't really argue with me.

That entire day, all 10 hours of driving, was spent on the phone, trying to figure out where Chris could go for treatment. We learned pretty quickly that you have to go to a separate detox place before the treatment centers would even take you.

We also learned that these treatment centers came with a high, high price tag that we were in no position to pay.

So many choices my head was spinning. Detox place then treatment place. Detox and treatment together at the same place. 30 days? 60 days? 90 days?

And then there were the price tags to these places—$30, 40, 50 grand—and here we were, looking to get me better on a budget.

Through the guidance of Cole, a counselor friend of my brother's, we decided on a detox place first, and then we would work out long-term treatment.

I know I mentioned earlier in the book that my dad was a bit "cold" to Chris at the beginning of our relationship, but it hadn't taken him long to accept him and treat him as one of the family. He was always available to give good advice and guidance throughout the years to both Chris and me.

The detox center that had an opening for Chris, starting that very night, charged $3,500 for 13 days, which might as well have been $3 million dollars to us at the time. And they wanted CASH up front—there was no payment plan. And they definitely did not take insurance.

With a phone call, my dad had a check waiting for us the minute we got back into the state of Oklahoma. I can't even express the relief I felt picking up that check. It might have been just money to anyone else, but to us, it meant Chris getting his LIFE back.

I can never ever thank Susie's dad, Terry, enough for the unconditional love and support he has shown me throughout the years.

*   *   *

We went home first so Chris could pack the stuff the detox center had requested he bring. He got to hug and kiss the kids and then we were right back in the car and headed towards the treatment center. I wasn't going to give him any time to change his mind.

As I reflect back on this time, it is pretty foggy, but certain memories have come back over time. I remember sitting across a desk from a heavy-set guy who seemed a bit threatening as he warned me that NOTHING could come into the detox center that was not on their approved list. He said my "things" would be thoroughly searched, and I said to him with a chuckle, "Does this include a body cavity search?"

He was not amused.

He opened up my toiletry kit to find the Valium that was prescribed to me in the hospital in Alabama, laughed, and said, "Well, these are definitely not going in." I told him I should probably take one because my anxiety was off the charts. He said, "One is probably not going to help you for what you are about to experience. You should probably take 3 or 4."

So, I did.

Little did I know, this would be the **LAST** time that I would abuse any drug or alcohol for the rest of my life.

*   *   *

As I climbed into my car in the parking lot of the detox center, all of the emotions from the past few days came to a head, and I just laid my head against the steering wheel and cried and cried. I had been trying to be so strong for Chris, to make him believe that everything would be okay, that HE would be okay, but at this point, let's be real, I didn't know if he would be. If *we* would be.

What if the detox center didn't work? What if he left it? What would I do? He couldn't come home and be like this in front of the kids! I couldn't let him drive the kids and put them in danger. So many unknowns, so many fears, and I was ... alone.

ALONE.

I knew when I got home that I'd have to put on a brave face for the kids. I knew that meals, homework, sporting commitments, all the normal "mom-duties," were all waiting for me. I remember finally stopping crying, wiping off my face, pulling my shoulders back and telling myself, "Susie. You are going to be fine. You've got this. You are STRONG and you have GOD on your side."

And then I drove home.

And to be completely honest, I was so relieved to have left Chris there. I felt relief that trained professionals were looking after him. I felt immense relief that he was finally, for a time at least, *safe*.

CHAPTER TWELVE

THE DAY I WOKE UP DEAD

I AWOKE, BUT could not seem to get my eyes opened. They felt glued shut.

And my hands, they felt like they weighed 1000 pounds each. I couldn't lift them. Actually, I couldn't even move my body.

And my mouth, my gosh, parched doesn't even begin to tell the story—someone had taken my mouth out, left it in the desert for three weeks and put it back in, dry and cracked.

And why was I sweating like this? Every pore in my body was oozing sweat.

What was happening to me? Did I die?

Was I ... DEAD?

Is this the day I woke up DEAD??

Can you actually wake up dead??

But then ... there were noises. A strange humming noise of some kind of machinery, and then I heard a door click loudly open and a woman's voice say, "Everybody up—time for vitals."

So, who was this lady, and why did she want my vitals??

I finally managed to open my eyes a little and, although things were blurry, I started to survey the room and I realized I wasn't dead. Whew. I think? But ... I definitely wasn't at home. And I wasn't on my parents' couch. Where in the heck was I? As I looked around, I realized the room was full of bunk beds. I looked up and sure enough, I was staring at the bottom of the bunk above me!

Everybody started to crawl out of their beds, and it was then I realized they were all wearing matching orange jumpsuits. Were they in PRISON?? Was I in prison??? I looked down and sure enough, I matched them! I wonder what they did?! Oh my gosh, I wonder what I did?!

As we started to march into a single file line as requested by the vitals-yelling lady, I turned and asked a fellow orange jumpsuiter, "Where the heck are we, and why am I here?"

The guy turned to me with a tired expression and said, "Welcome to Detox Hell."

Detox? Ohhhhhhhh, detox.

All of a sudden, bits and pieces of the day before started coming back to me. My previous week-long drunken journey followed by Susie picking me up and bringing me here came at me with a force. I felt like I was going to be sick. I told the vitals lady, "I'm going to be sick!" She nonchalantly pointed toward the trash can and I proceeded to "call the dinosaurs." You know, dinosaurs? They make the roaring sound?

Anyways, that's what it sounded like as I puked my guts up.

After I puked (with no apparent concern from anybody in the room), the vitals lady yelled at me, "Wipe it off and get back in line."

I looked at the clock and realized it was only 3 a.m.

3 A.M.???

Couldn't vitals wait until a normal time like 6 or 7 a.m.? How vital could the vitals be???

Next, they made us get in a single-file line and took us to a room with two desks, the kind you sit at in high school, each one manned by a nurse who was going to take our blood pressure, pulse and temperature. So, basically, when it was your turn, you were ON STAGE as you got your vitals taken.

Now might be a good time to remind you all of my special condition of "White Coat Fever," courtesy of the time I almost died at age 17.

When my blood pressure reading came back, the nurses looked at each other, and one said to the other, "Do it again." So, she took it again. Based on her reaction, it must have been all kinds of whacked out. From that point on, the nurses and my fellow orange jumpsuiters all started calling me "the high blood pressure guy."

The guys would literally chant, "No Whammies" every time the nurses would take my blood pressure. If it came back too high, the nurses wouldn't let me move on, and everyone would groan and feel bad for me because it was apparently a "whammy"!

Once I finally passed, they let us go back to bed until a few hours later when they would wake us up and it happened all over again. Imagine how excited I was to find out that I would get to be "on stage" getting my BP taken four times a day for the next 13 days, all while experiencing the worst sweats, shakes, trembling, stomach cramps you could imagine and facing the reality of the nightmare I've caused for everyone ... all while hearing the ongoing chant of "No Whammies."

*   *   *

I started hearing other orange jumpsuiters refer to me and a handful of others as "Privateers." At first, I just assumed it meant I was a "new guy," but I soon came to realize that 90% of the people were court-ordered to be there. They called me a privateer because I had volunteered, or apparently Susie volunteered me, to be there and even paid the $3,500 for detox.

Apparently, this put me in the category of a "chump" in their eyes. I even started hearing murmurs that I might be some kind of undercover cop. Then they got bolder. "Hey, are you a narc?"

I guess they didn't think I fit the mold of what a guy in detox should look like.

*   *   *

Let's be really, really clear here—addiction has no boundaries. There is no "type" immune to this awful disease. No income class, no race, no religious upbringing, no amount of education—

EVERYBODY is a potential candidate for the awful disease of addiction.

*   *   *

No visitors were allowed, but Susie could drop off care packages that were, of course, searched. Not that Susie would sneak me in any contraband. In fact, she probably packed me the healthiest snacks of any inmates ... I mean, residents.

I was allowed one phone call per day, which I looked forward to with eager anticipation, for it often led to an update of what was going on with the kids and Susie at home. At the same time, I can also remember feeling really anxious about this phone call because I knew my being in this place was not helping with our already disastrous financial situation. But ... I also knew that I had no choice BUT to be there, so it was a bit of a helpless feeling.

The very next morning, Chris called me. I remember answering the phone, practically holding my breath, because I just knew he was going to tell me to come get him. That he couldn't stay there. And I knew that I was going to have to tell him "No" for his own well-being.

Surprisingly, he was only calling to ask me to bring him a few things. Whew. I was so relieved.

I got the requested items together, drove the 30 minutes to the detox center to drop them off (no visitors, of course), and headed back home.

My phone rang and it was my daughter, very upset and babbling on about our dog bleeding everywhere. I assured her I would be there as fast as possible and hurried home, wondering what emergency I was going to have to deal with next.

Turns out our dog had cut her ear, and guess what? Dog's ears spurt massive amounts of blood everywhere.

My son, Carson, had tried to handle it but … there was blood EVERYWHERE. Have you ever tried to fasten a dog ear splint??? If not, it's incredibly tricky.

So, I dealt with that mess and then had to race Macy to a gymnastics meet. While at the meet, I just remember looking around at all the smiling people and thinking how nice it must be to not be worried about your husband fighting for his very life in detox or to be worried about your entire future and how you would possibly be able to support all four kiddos if your spouse couldn't get better.

I felt… alone. Alone and afraid.

But I sat there smiling and clapping and acting like life was fine. Later that evening, I was at a baseball game for my youngest son, Maddox, and everyone was once again … happy. *Carefree*. They would ask me, "Where's Chris?" And I'm sure I smiled and said, "Out of town" or something. Once again, I sat there acting like everything in my world was good. Because falling off the bleachers into a sobbing puddle on the ground and rocking in the fetal position probably would've been frowned upon.

You know that quote, "Be kinder than necessary because you don't know what battle someone is fighting?" Well, yep, that was me during this time. I was fighting a battle for my family's very existence, but nobody would've known it from my actions or attitude. These are the personal times that taught me firsthand that you never know what someone is actually going through, so err on the side of *kindness*.

*   *   *

So I quickly settled into a daily routine of vitals four times per day and the rest of the time was spent trying to grasp a new reality without mind-altering substances to numb any stress, pain or feelings. This might sound weird if you've never been addicted to a mind-altering substance, but I realized that I was starting to experience all types of emotions. Sadness, happiness, anger, depression, happiness again, excitement about the future, fear of the future ... and so on and so forth.

For so long, the alcohol and pain pills had numbed any and all of my emotions so much that I was really taken by surprise when I started having allllll the feelings. And these feelings were coming hard and fast.

The vital checks were followed by "groups." These groups were basically where we would share our addictions and what had gotten us to this point. It was basically a huge commiseration of what brought us to the detox place. We were served some really crappy food, but it didn't really matter as I wasn't hungry anyways. I was way too busy experiencing the worst sweats, trembles, body cramps, aches, mind racing and restlessness. Take the flu, put it on steroids times ten thousand, and you're still not even close to the amount of pain and discomfort I was in.

*   *   *

The one thing that started to give me some peace was reading some Bible scriptures. Remember Cole? The guy that helped coordinate my getting into this detox place? He had sent me some Bible scriptures on my phone that I had hurriedly scribbled on the side of a Styrofoam cup before they took my phone away. Susie had packed my Bible, and I started diving into it like I never had before.

Now, during these years of full-blown addiction, I still prayed, and we went to church. Shoot, we even served in the church. Susie was a greeter and I was a golf cart driver. We go to a big church, so I drove around the parking lot and picked people up to save them from having to walk very far. So ... if I ever drove YOU in the cart, congrats, you arrived safe and sound!

But, seriously, I always had great intentions during that time to grow closer to Christ but it's tough to do when you're in a committed relationship with alcohol and pills.

*   *   *

While Chris was at the detox center, my oldest son came home from his baseball trip—the one Chris had driven to in Florida. He knew that Chris had "gotten sick" and left Florida, but I had shielded him from the harsh reality so that he wouldn't worry while playing in his school tournament. I remember sitting him and Carson down on one of their beds, taking a deep breath, and telling them that their dad was in a detox center.

I don't exactly know what all was said, but I'll never forget them asking, "What if he doesn't get better?" I just remember sitting there, trying not to cry, and telling them that I just didn't know. I didn't know what was going to happen.

I could tell my two littles that daddy was sick and in a place that was helping him get better, but my older two were teenagers. They could not be placated with a generalized "butterflies and rainbows" answer. They had watched Chris get sober the first time, and they had been watching him go downhill fast this time. I just had to be honest and tell them that I wasn't sure what was going to happen, but that we were all going to pray like never before and trust that the Lord would heal Chris and take care of us all.

All of these things—the dog's ear emergency, the gymnastics meet, Maddox's baseball game, the serious convo with the older boys—these were all things that Chris would've either handled or been a part of with me.

And he wasn't there. He was in detox.

If he had been fighting any other disease besides addiction, I would've told people what we were going through and they would've been bringing me casseroles and offering to help out with the kids. But not with the disease of addiction. It is a lonely, lonely disease, both for the addict and for their loved ones. It is truly a family disease because everyone is affected and everyone suffers.

But there is HOPE. And that's what I want to tell you about next.

CHAPTER THIRTEEN

WHY ME?

THIS IS WHERE I need your full, undivided attention. What I'm about to tell you changed everything for me, and my hope is that by sharing this, if you or someone you know is struggling with addiction, they might be able to follow the same path that has led me to complete freedom from any desire to drink or do any kind of drugs.

A complete FREEDOM from addiction.

On the fifth morning of my stay at the detox center, I found myself reading some of the scriptures that my buddy Cole had shared, in hope that they would give me some clarity.

James 1:12 "Blessed is the one who perseveres under trial because, having stood the test, that person will receive the crown of life that the Lord has promised to those who love him."

Joshua 1:9 "Have I not commanded you? Be strong and courageous. Do not be afraid; do not be discouraged, for the Lord your God will be with you wherever you go."

Galatians 2:20 "I have been crucified with Christ and I no longer live, but Christ lives in me. The life I now live in the body, I live by faith in the Son of God, who loved me and gave himself for me."

Romans 8:38-39 "For I am convinced that neither death nor life, neither angels nor demons, neither the present nor the future, nor any powers, neither height nor depth, nor anything else in all creation, will be able to separate us from the love of God that is in Christ Jesus our Lord."

As I was reading and re-reading these scriptures, I found myself on my knees, my Bible open in front of me, surrounded by bunk beds, in a very vulnerable, intimate, transparent conversation with God.

With tears rolling down my face, I said a very specific prayer that a former detox resident, who had years of sobriety under his belt and had come to one of my group sessions, had told us he prayed.

With all the humility in the world, knowing that I was broken and lost and didn't want to stay that way, I prayed, "Lord, please wrap your Holy Spirit around me and remove any and all desire to drink or take pills from me."

As soon as I said that prayer, I felt the darkness lift from me, and I knew right then and there, without a shadow of a doubt, that HE had done as I asked. At the very moment I completed that prayer, I was FREE.

To be clear, I didn't see rays of light coming from heaven with a choir of singing angels or hear the audible voice of God, but I felt an indescribable sensation and I knew at that very moment that I had been set FREE. It was like God had taken this incredible darkness that had been cast over me for so long and replaced it with a light that only He can give.

Now, time out. I'm not whack-a-doo.

I don't go around talking like this. As a matter of fact, when other people say things like this, it always sounds a bit hokey. I'm a skeptic by nature, so if you are skeptical, I get it.

I'm not discounting others' experiences, but sometimes when people say things like, "The Holy Ghost said I should have pepperoni not cheese," I get a little cynical. So, when I tell you this happened, I'm not saying it lightly.

So if you are cynical like me, I get it. But this ... this was a movement of God. This was an ACT of GOD. It's not like I hadn't prayed over and over before this moment but this was the first time I prayed with a heart of full SURRENDER. It's not that the words of the prayer were "magical," it's the fact that I was praying it for the first time with the clarity of mind that I had absolutely NO CONTROL to stop abusing alcohol and drugs on my own and that I was completely 100% dependent upon God's saving grace.

After this miracle "release," I knew I could walk out the front door of the detox center right then and there and never touch drugs or alcohol again as long as I lived. The DESIRE was gone. The "darkness"—the trap—the place that I had been stuck ... was now gone. And in its place was LIGHT.

I literally was jumping up and down for joy because He had done it. He lifted the darkness from me and, clear as day, I could tell right then that He had released me.

Christ had just acted on my behalf and it shook me.

Gratitude doesn't even begin to describe how I felt. No words can adequately express just how I was feeling at this time.

*   *   *

Once the shock of what had just happened started to wear off, I asked myself, "Why me? Why did the Lord do this for **ME**?" I mean, this place is full of people just like me that need Him and need this same miracle release. I'm literally walking through the detox center of the walking dead and wondering, "Why me, God, and not all of them?"

And I strongly believe that THIS—this book—me, sharing my story with all of you—is THE REASON that He answered my prayer that day.

So that I could tell all of you that there is HOPE in CHRIST.

That Christ can set you free from any and all chains of bondage.

I am not looking to become the poster child for sobriety, but I am looking to be the poster child for Christ's saving grace.

*   *   *

So, there I was in detox, realizing that I didn't even need to be there anymore! God had just HEALED ME. Let me say that again ...

GOD. HAD. JUST. HEALED. ME.

But... even with this newfound revelation of freedom, I was level-headed enough to realize that I had one big problem. There wasn't anybody, and I mean ANYBODY, that was going to believe me. I had spent the last decade of my life lying, manipulating, disguising ... all so I could feed my habit. Why would anyone believe my story of being "healed," when I was stuck in detox hell? How convenient! How many times have they heard someone say, "GOD healed me—I'm good!" And then the guy left and walked to the nearest bar?

There I was, all healed and stuff, but still in detox, and although I KNEW I didn't need it anymore, nobody there was going to agree with me. Certainly, Ms. Vitals Nurse who kicked in my door every morning at 3 a.m. was not suddenly going to say, "Well, good golly, Chris, you just sleep in since you got all the healing!"

So, I continued to go through the daily routines, but secretly, I was whispering to my bunkmates what had happened and that they maybe should try it for themselves. I wanted everybody to experience the freedom that I was experiencing.

They all looked at me like I was a little crazy, but a few of them tried it. I even followed up months later with one of them, and he was sober as a nun!

*   *   *

As I started nearing the end of my stay in detox, the staff started wanting to talk about rehab. And I knew that any rehab place I went to was going to come with a hefty price tag of dollars that we didn't have to spare.

Chris called me and told me that he was nearing the end of his 10-day stay and that I needed to come down to talk to the counselors about the next step. My response? "**10** days!! You are supposed to stay there **13** days!!" I did NOT want him to leave early. We paid the $3,500, and I wanted to get every second we could! He went on to assure me that he was good—he PROMISED—and that we would talk about everything when I got there.

Things were ramping up. Susie was coming to sit down with my counselors to discuss treatment options of 30 days, 60 days, 90 days and even a year. Treatment options that cost a minimum of $25,000 upward to a $100,000. Obviously, that is the normal progression—detox and then rehab.

There I was, stressing about all of these options, knowing all the while that I didn't even NEED them! But, there was NO TRUST. I wasn't even sure I got a vote. EVERYBODY, including Susie and the PROFESSIONALS, thought I needed to go to REHAB, and they thought I needed to go for a minimum of 90 days.

I decided that I was going to have to tell Susie what had happened. With everything I had dragged her through, I knew this wasn't going to be easy and certainly wouldn't sound believable. And that she would either (a) think it was a total crock, or (b) believe me.

If she didn't believe me, I knew I would just have to do the time at rehab even though I knew I didn't need it. I was willing to go, although it meant the Lord would have to once again perform a miracle because $25,000 was a LOT of money, especially when you didn't have any.

*   *   *

TIME OUT. I don't want anyone to think that, somehow, I'm suggesting rehab is not a good idea ... because **IT IS.**

Rehab is a GREAT IDEA and truly the only answer for many, many people. I've helped other people suffering from addiction find sobriety, and the help they desperately needed came from rehab.

Rehab is a place to be able to slowly adapt to a world without substances to mask your feelings and emotions. Rehab is a place where you learn HOW to deal with said feelings and emotions. Rehab is a place that helps you find yourself again, all while letting your body and brain heal from years of alcohol and/or drug abuse.

*   *   *

But back to MY story. So, Susie came to the detox center, and she and a counselor sat down with me. I remember asking her if she liked the particular shade of orange jumpsuit I was wearing or the lighter shade of the one I had on the last time she saw me. She was only mildly amused.

But it was time to get down to biz.

We started discussing an aftercare program with the counselor, and he started laying out the different options. It was at that moment that I asked the counselor to step out so I could have a private convo with Susie.

So, I told her.

I told her what had happened. I told her about the prayer and the crazy miracle that I had experienced. But I followed that by telling her that I would go to any treatment place. This wasn't me trying to manipulate—I wanted her to know that I would do what I needed to do. I let her know that I understood if she didn't believe or trust me.

If she said, GO, I would go.

It was weird talking to a very coherent Chris. I hadn't seen him this clear-headed in quite some time. When he told me that he didn't need to go to rehab, I was instantly skeptical and ready to fight tooth and nail that he would be going—no ifs, ands or buts. I had no idea how we were going to pay for it, but I was trusting the Lord would provide. Not going to rehab was not even an option I had considered for him. However, when he started explaining what had happened while praying for the Lord to wrap the Holy Spirit around him and the subsequent "release" from darkness that he felt, I got chills all over my whole body. He was so emotional while trying to explain it to me that I believed every word he said, with my *heart* at least.

My *mind*, however, was struggling to accept his story because I had become so accustomed to him lying and manipulating situations that I had put up walls and learned NOT to trust him.

But I did sense something really different about him, and a small glimmer of HOPE started beckoning me to believe him. And I wanted nothing more in the world than for him to be healed of this awful disease that had completely ruled and ruined our lives up to this point.

After a lengthy discussion, we decided I could go home with her that day, and we'd pray and ask for the Lord's guidance for the next step. All with the understanding that I would find AA meetings to attend every single day while we were developing a long-term plan.

I was fine with that! I was going HOME!

CHAPTER FOURTEEN

HOW GODRONIC!!

I WILL NEVER forget that car ride home from detox. I was so happy to have my best friend back with me. He was the Chris that I had always known, the pre-addiction Chris. He was clear-eyed, smiling and as funny as all get out.

THIS was the guy I had fallen in love with all those years back in Social Problems! This was the guy that was an incredible provider and leader for our family. This was the guy that loved me and the kids more than life itself.

I was cautiously filled with hope that he was back for good.

Wow, the emotions.

The feelings.

Everything FELT.

I had numbed my emotions and feelings for so long that it was weird to try and process normal feelings. Going through tough financial times, I numbed them. Sad times, I numbed them. Scared times, I numbed them. Heck, I even numbed happy times. I had become a professional at suppressing my feelings by covering them with alcohol and drugs.

I felt like I was a newborn when it came to experiencing feelings because EVERY LITTLE THING caused me to FEEL my feelings.

It felt GOOD to feel my feelings ... except for the bad feelings. The shame, the pain, the reality that I had crashed and burned was still difficult to deal with.

And FEAR. Fear that I would fail. What if I was wrong about everything and God hadn't really healed me?

And so many questions. I mean I had been isolated in a very structured environment where 100% of my focus and time was spent on me and my sobriety. So now I was going home to fill the many roles of father, husband, provider, protector—but how would I handle it? Was Susie going to wake me up at 3 a.m. and check my vitals?? How would we know my vitals if she didn't??

*   *   *

One of the first things we did upon arriving home was to take our two dogs on a walk. It has always been one of our things to do together. The kids were at school, so it gave us a bit of time to acclimate him to being home again. Everything I had read had warned me that it's critical to keep their stress low upon coming home from detox or rehab, so I was working hard to make that happen. The whole "one day at a time" thing. I remember on that walk holding his hand and him telling me, "I am just so incredibly GRATEFUL. I cannot explain to you the GRATITUDE that I feel." And the way he said it ... well, I get chills remembering it to this very day.

Grateful doesn't begin to tell the story. I felt so incredibly free that I swore I would never let a day go by without expressing my gratitude. I had been in such a dark place for so long, and I knew the only reason I was home, walking in the sunshine with my beautiful wife, was because Christ had saved me from my addiction. Christ had given me another chance, and I wasn't going to screw it up. With this chance also came an incredible sense of OBLIGATION to help other people.

*   *   *

Once back at the house, I begin leading Susie on a "parade" around the house, de-alcoholing all of my hidey holes. Water bottles filled with vodka instead of water ... Gatorade bottles under my spare tire ... beer cans stashed in the attic ... pill bottles tucked in my underwear drawer ... all kinds of things I had stashed in case I had a need for it.

He really was a changed person. I felt so happy. I remember telling him we needed to immediately find AA meetings for him to go to and he agreed. When he drove off to go to the first meeting alone, I started to panic. What if he stopped at 7-Eleven and got a beer? What if he didn't go to AA at all? I remember having to take deep breaths and remind myself that I wasn't in control of him and that all I could do was pray—so I did.

Susie agreed that I didn't need to go to rehab because she could sense the genuine change in me. We both felt at peace with that decision.

*   *   *

Life slowly started to return to normal. Stress crept back in, especially financial stress. But Chris continued to do well. I have to be honest, I worried and fretted and, although I would "give it to God," I would end up taking it right back.

But, the more time that went by, the less guarded I became. Trust isn't earned back quickly—trust is earned back over time and with evidence that it is deserved. Chris was working hard to earn it back.

We did take appropriate measures to protect his sobriety. We separated ourselves from chaos. We distanced ourselves from negativity. We became careful about who and what we let influence our lives. We did everything in our power to PROTECT OUR PEACE. And something I learned during this time is that not everyone will like your choices, not everyone will understand your choices, but that's okay, they are YOUR choices.

It was once again, and honestly more than ever, Chris & Susie Against the World, only this time we were sure to include God.

*   *   *

In that time period of humble evaluation, I had decided to change my priorities in life completely. I was no longer going to worry about what others thought. I was no longer going to worry about how much money we were or weren't making. I was going to stop doing life to impress other people, but instead live my life to impress the Lord and be true to myself. The opinions of others no longer mattered to me.

This evaluation even affected how I made a living. I decided I was going to try and find something that was less stressful and more fulfilling.

The Lord orchestrated a deal where we were able to buy a fishing company. We loved the outdoors and felt this would be a perfect family biz. We did this for a while and honestly thought we would do it forever but ... God.

God had different plans. Bigger, crazier plans then we could've ever imagined.

He dropped an incredible opportunity into our lives that completely changed everything for us. My health, our finances—so unbelievably God's plan that we still pinch ourselves daily to remind ourselves that this is our real life.

A health and wellness company. How amazingly funny is God? Just to show how in control HE is, he takes one of the most unlikely, unhealthy candidates alive and transforms him into one of the biggest health advocates on the planet!! How GODRONIC!! There honestly is no reasonable explanation for what has happened in our lives other than GOD.

*   *   *

And here I am, coming up on SIX years of being sober. From that day that I wondered if God really healed me—from that day—not once have I had any desire, not even an ounce, to drink or do any kind of drugs.

So, if you are reading this and wondering what your life could look like without drinking or pills, I'm here to tell you that it can be the most wonderful, fulfilling life that you didn't even know was possible to live.

It doesn't have to be the feeling of "missing out"—I've never felt that way. I've never felt deprived. As a matter of fact, you'll begin to appreciate the new feelings and emotions so much that you will never want to risk going back to the dark place. You can experience an inner peace and joy so great that you will never regret living a life of sobriety.

CHAPTER FIFTEEN

THERE'S ALWAYS HOPE

THE DISEASE OF ADDICTION is not picky. It can happen to anyone. We wanted you to see what our family life was like and how this disease creeps up on you and then progresses to a point of life-threatening destruction. About 43% of adults in the US (76 million people) have had a parent, child, sibling or spouse who is or was an alcoholic.[1] According to the National Survey on Drug Use and Health (NSDUH), 21.5 million American adults (aged 12 and older) battled a substance use disorder in 2014.[2] Trust me, if I could just make everyone in the world not ever drink alcohol or take any kind of drugs, I would do so to save you all from this potential pain. Because you never know who "it" is going to choose next. The disease of addiction doesn't care how old or young, how rich or poor, how educated or uneducated, how spiritual or unspiritual... EVERYONE is fair game to this sneaky disease.

If you are currently fighting addiction, it's important that you know I have been where you

---

[1] http://www.alcoholism-statistics.com/family-statistics
[2] https://www.samhsa.gov/data/sites/default/files/NSDUH-FRR1-2014/NSDUH-FRR1-2014.pdf

are. I need you to accept that I was at the lowest of the lows. I was as bad as, or worse than, anyone struggling with addiction.

You have to know that YOUR PROBLEM can't be worse than mine was because my next step was ... DEATH.

So if you are reading this thinking, "Well, he just doesn't understand how bad I am," it's critical that you know I do!! **I DO** understand! I know where you or your loved one is at.

But the DESIRE has to be yours. Notice that you never hear a recovering addict say, "You know, I quit because my wife or my mom wanted me to."

ZERO times you will ever hear that.

*   *   *

Throughout our journey, we've learned some major lessons that we want to share with people who are either in the battle themselves or have a loved one facing this lonely battle of addiction.

The first lesson is that the person fighting the addiction is the ONLY person who can make the decision to STOP. You cannot want it FOR them. Your love for them and your desire for them to stop is not enough. You can guide them down the right path towards help, but your desire for them to stop will never be enough. It has to be THEM.

Now, here is the tricky part. If someone is so foggy-headed and whacked out of their mind that they are incapable of making a logical decision, you will need to steer them in the direction of help. They are not of sound mind to make these kinds of decisions. You'll have to do the best you can to point them in the right direction. Some states have even recently passed laws so that family members can check loved ones into rehabilitation programs without their permission.

Now I'm here to tell you, for years, there was nothing in the world I wanted more than for Chris to get sober. However, it had to be HIS choice if we had any chance of him staying in recovery. Remember that first day home from detox, when I was worried about him stopping for liquor on the way to an AA meeting? Chris said something to me that day that I will never forget:

"Honey, I can stop anytime, anywhere and drink if I want to, but for the first time in my life, I have ZERO desire to do it. And it has to be ME making that decision, not you. You have no control."

And I knew right then that he was right. If I had any control at all, he would've stopped drinking years earlier!

*   *   *

The next major lesson we learned is that everybody's journey through addiction and their path to recovery is going to look different.

For some, it will be a detox center followed by an inpatient rehabilitation program of 30, 60, 90 or more days. Some need a full year. Some will need to follow this by living in a sober living house for a certain period of time. For some it will be attending daily AA (Alcoholics Anonymous) or NA (Narcotics Anonymous) meetings. Some will find their help in weekly Celebrate Recovery meetings. Some will need sponsors and some will need mentors. Some will get sober and then relapse six times before they finally are in recovery for good.

But we believe that for every one of these paths, there is one good starting place, and that is the prayer I mentioned earlier. (If you are not a believer, get yourself a Bible and read the verses that I laid out earlier and say a simple prayer inviting Jesus into your heart.)

The exact prayer that someone taught me and that I want YOU to pray is:

"Dear Heavenly Father, please wrap the HOLY SPIRIT around me and take away any desire to drink or do drugs."

I remember telling this to a buddy of mine who was struggling with addiction, and he said, very sarcastically, "Oh Great, Chris, **this** is your plan? I'm over here jamming needles into my arms, and your plan is for me to say a prayer?"

He wanted nothing more than to be clean and sober, so he said the prayer, and after a 90-day rehabilitation program, he is still sober today, three years later.

Not only did I say this prayer back then, I say it every single day and will continue to do so the rest of my life. And remember the KEY to this prayer being effective is the connection between your heart and the words - full SURRENDER to God. Full SURRENDER to acknowledging that you do not have control over the addiction in your life.

Listen, if you're not the addict but the loved one of an addict, you are going to insert their name into that prayer. Pray the prayer FOR them.

"Dear Heavenly Father, please wrap the Holy Spirit around _____ and take away any desire he/she has to drink or do drugs."

I will tell you, I have never prayed so much in my life as I did during those years of Chris's addiction. And the Lord, although not on *my* timeline, was completely FAITHFUL.

*   *   *

The next MAJOR lesson we have learned is that you need to PROTECT YOUR PEACE.

What do I mean by that? Whatever you need to do to stay in recovery, do it. You will have to separate yourself from certain people. This does not mean that you don't love them or care for them. It just means that you are choosing to LIVE.

There will be people who are threatened by your newfound sobriety and, if you're good at being addicted, you'll have surrounded yourself with many other addicts to whom your usage of mind altering substances just seems normal. So, you will have to separate yourself from these people because your sobriety will threaten their own addiction. They might even try to persuade you that "you could have just one beer, dude."

Listen, there's a popular saying that I agree with wholeheartedly: "One beer is too many, and one hundred is not enough." I've often said I'm not sure what I would rather have put in my mouth, a loaded pistol? or a beer? No Joke. Because one leads to a quick death while the latter leads to a slow death of pain and destruction, not just for me but for all of those that I love dearly.

I want you to do an inventory of the people you have in your life. Are there people who are constantly in chaos? They seem to thrive on drama or drama just seems to follow them around? You need to avoid these people and love them from a safe distance because chaos will threaten your recovery. Chaos will give you an excuse to dive off the sobriety train real fast.

PROTECT YOUR PEACE.

There will be places and activities that you need to avoid, at least for a certain amount of time, because they can be triggers for your addiction.

Take me, for example. Every time I played golf, I also drank a 12-pack of beer. Of course, this was just for the first 9 holes, and then I'd start buying from the cart girl for the back 9. I didn't play golf for YEARS when I was first in recovery, but I can go play golf now, no problem.

Maybe for you, it's a certain restaurant that triggers you wanting to drink. Don't go there. Or maybe it's a certain town that you always stopped in at a particular liquor store. Don't go through that town! Find an alternate route. Maybe it's a particular style of music or a particular song on the radio? Dude, just change the station.

PROTECT YOUR PEACE.

Even though I knew upon leaving the detox center that I was completely free from the desire to drink or do drugs, I was still extremely cautious about potential triggers that I may not have anticipated being a problem.

Be smart and PROTECT YOUR PEACE.

*   *   *

Just as important as who and what you separate yourself from is who and what you SURROUND yourself with. The activities you partake in on a daily basis will impact your sobriety.

Exercising is a great choice as it is positive and actually leads to a physical release of endorphins, which you will want and need as you start this new way of living sober. Plus, you are going to be amazed at how great you feel, and you will become proud of yourself, the stronger you become.

Building back our self-worth is critically important in the beginning stages of recovery. Running, weight-lifting, hiking outdoors, yoga, CrossFit, group fitness classes—any of these activities will provide you with both physical and mental support. Finding a group of people who also enjoy these activities is even better because it's never good for a recovering addict to isolate themselves. There are some amazing communities of support and encouragement that you can become a part of—people who are all looking to better themselves and live a happier, healthier life of freedom.

*   *   *

Next, please know that you do not have to go through this ALONE.

For so long, people have been ashamed to speak of addiction because it is looked at as a "defect" not a disease. Thankfully I feel that society as a whole is becoming more educated on the subject of addiction, the disease, which is helping to break the stigma associated with it. In turn, people will feel much more comfortable reaching out for help and support.

Nobody should have to go thru this alone. There are support groups for both the addicts and the family and friends of the addict. There are even Facebook groups! There is a pretty new social media movement amongst the younger generation of glamorizing being sober. And of being open about addiction and recovery. I love it.

*   *   *

There is HOPE.

Hope.

I now live my daily life without any desire to drink or take pills. And it is a more incredible, fulfilling life then I ever could've dreamed.

My fear is that people will think they have to hide and stay in the fetal position once they get sober. That all the fun in life is over. But that's exactly the OPPOSITE of what actually happens. You are no longer a slave. You are no longer held captive by your addiction. You won't have to fight cravings off every minute of every day, not with the HOLY SPIRIT wrapped around you. I've truly had more FUN in the past six years of life then I had for the previous twenty!

There is hope for a marriage being affected by addiction.

I'm not going to tell you it's easy, but it's possible. We had a counselor tell us that he was very surprised we managed to stay married through Chris's years of addiction because most don't. Most lose their marriage, their children, their houses, their jobs.

Addiction takes and takes and takes. But it doesn't have to.

Remember how it's always been Chris and Susie (& now God!) Against the World? Well, in this case, it is no different. If he couldn't go someplace or be around a group of people because they might threaten his recovery, then I wouldn't either. It really has always been a simple decision for me.

Chris's LIFE is more important to me and our family than any other group of people or any places. If you are the spouse or loved one of the addict, the SUPPORT you give them will be critical to their recovery success. Plus, as I tell Chris daily, he's super lucky to have married the most incredible wife evaaaaaa!!!

> **There is hope** for relationships to be restored. People are amazingly forgiving when they are asked. So, ASK forgiveness. And if you are not the addict, give forgiveness when asked. Remember that your loved one was not of sound mind and now they are. Forgive.

> **There is hope** for the return of joy in your life.

> **There is hope** for laughter, happiness and fulfillment.

> Ultimately **there is HOPE** in CHRIST.

*   *   *

Romans 8:28 is one of my very favorite verses in the Bible. It says that, in ALL THINGS, God works for the good of those who love Him. I love this verse so much because it shows us that no matter what dumb choices WE MAKE, God can use those choices for our ultimate good. How incredibly awesome is that? God can turn our struggles into His triumph.

> I am one of the lucky ones. There are so many people walking around in a hazy, booze-filled or pain-pill-filled fog, not really living their lives. These people THINK they are the lucky ones because they are FUNCTIONING. I'm here to tell you, I'm the lucky one. I thank God that I crashed and burned. Because I now live every day fully present, filled with joy and gratitude.

*   *   *

By sharing our struggles through addiction, we are hopeful that you can learn from our experiences and not feel alone or shameful.

During the past six years of sobriety, God has taken us on a very unexpected journey where we have been put in the position to have a large social media following and we live our lives very OUT LOUD. We are as transparent as they come.

And yet, as open and honest as we live our lives, *this* message had to be way more than just a random Facebook live. We needed to take you down the entire path for you to understand where we've been and *why we are who we are* today.

If there is one thing we want you to take away from this book, it's that no matter how dark, how extreme, how out of control your or your loved one's addiction may be, there is always

HOPE.

ABOUT THE AUTHORS

Chris and Susie McColl are popular social media figures who live life out loud to the fullest. Genuine and transparent, they preach a message of gratitude, positivity and faith. They love to make others laugh all while inspiring them to pursue their dreams.

Their mission in life, after going through a life and death battle with addiction, is to help others live a happier, healthier life of FREEDOM.

After meeting in a class called "Social Problems" at the University of Oklahoma, they have been happily married (most of the time!) for 26 years and have four kids, Tanner, Carson, Maddox & Macy, who are the loves of their lives. They love the outdoors, fitness and health, and especially their three German Shorthaired Pointers, Wilson, Shyla and Daisy. They are fortunate enough to work together from home growing their social marketing business.

To learn more about the McColls and their mission, go to: www.thedayIwokeupdead.com or follow them on Facebook & Instagram at Chris McColl and Susie Fritts McColl.